Three Centuries of
FURNITURE

A STUDIO BOOK · THE VIKING PRESS · NEW YORK

Three Centuries of
FURNITURE

H. D. Molesworth and John Kenworthy-Browne

PREFATORY NOTE

Styles in furniture and decoration can seldom be very exactly defined—and certainly not readily fitted within convenient date spans. That does not, however, stop most of us from trying to do so. Occasionally an individual piece may be precisely datable, and thus afford firm evidence of the period and style; or, in later centuries, when the keeping of records became more detailed and reliable, some special innovations, and possibly designers or makers, may have been documented. But, by and large, each style grew out of something that had gone before; most styles continued for at least one generation—and many, particularly in the provinces, persisted over two or three or even more generations. Craftsmen were likely to continue for their whole lifetimes working along lines they had learned as apprentices and in the past, as now, many people continued to commission outmoded forms.

As a logical result of these tendencies, furniture styles run concurrently and interweave or overlap, both in time and place. This happens within individual countries and is even more evident when you are dealing with examples drawn from an entire continent. However international certain influences may have eventually become, the extent of their adoption or adaptation from one area to another has nearly always depended upon a host of social and political factors, including wars, religions, dynastic marriages, or even upon minor local squabbles or the tastes of personalities.

Because of all these considerations, we have attempted only to group the large number of color illustrations included in this book under certain rather arbitrary headings. As will be seen, this grouping arises from and is concerned with the essentials of a style rather than its geographical variants.

Contents

The Background

(Plates 1–60)

This introductory section seeks briefly to review the main lines in the development of domestic furniture in Europe from Gothic through Renaissance to baroque times. As is suggested in the opening essay, it would seem valid to make a distinction—at least of basic approach—between the countries of the North and those of the Mediterranean, and among these with Italy in particular. Thus the first three pages of illustrations (pp. 17–19) contrast a selection of solid Northern Gothic pieces with examples of the first type of Italian Renaissance. In broad terms, these are contemporary; and even with such a handful of examples the difference of approach is clear. The following pages have been divided between Southern and Northern productions. Much of the opening series concentrates on Italian developments of the 16th and early 17th centuries, since these were so much in advance of the rest of the Continent. The first few pages (20–21) show some of the elaborations that were quickly imposed upon the initial Renaissance forms; this was in keeping with the interest in classical studies. We have included the court taste of France with the Italian works here, since they were closely knit, though Gothic traces still persisted in outlying provinces. The next examples (pp. 22–27) show mainly how the inspiration of the Florentines came to be combined with traditional Gallic elegance, thus producing more or less the only other school of particular aesthetic distinction.

The decline in late-16th-century Italy (pp. 28–29) shows the same emphasis on elaboration (even to the point of fussiness), rather than the initial architectural dignity of line and form, that is manifest in the succeeding German examples (Plates 30–34). Turning to the North and elsewhere, we next give a sampling from England and America at about this time (Plates 35–48); in these one notes a continuance of oak and of basic sturdiness in the new Protestant areas. It would be foolish to insist, in such pieces, upon finding refinements that do not exist.

What happened to the Italianate baroque tradition in northern Italy and in other Catholic lands is manifest in the closing pages of this section (pp. 40–47). Rich, colorful, unashamedly showy and often rather coarse, this development laid the foundations of an approach for princely life in which any pleasant Gothic virtues such as a becoming modesty were thrown out the window. As we shall see, things were to remain much this way in Catholic Southern districts until our own century.

Among most of us, there is implanted the idea that the dawn of contemporary Western civilization came with "the Fall of the Roman Empire." It sounds well, and—as an easy generalization—this notion may have some validity, since it can reasonably be claimed that European culture depends to a large degree upon its Mediterranean heritage, which had survived in court circles and in ecclesiastical centers in spite of the invaders from the East. At the same time, to consider it more circumspectly, one should recall that the so-called "Fall" itself took several generations and that, by reasonable computation, another half millennium passed by (as long as from the time of Columbus to the present day) before any enduring order was established under feudalism. Even then, it took nearly as long again for any widespread domestic civilization to evolve. Furthermore, the invaders themselves, even after they had embraced Christianity and something of its heritage, still retained much of their own behavioral tradition. All these factors are germane to our subject.

One might say, for example, that there always have been and—even with the movements toward internationalism today—still are, deep-rooted differences of attitude between the robust individualistic peoples of the Mediterranean lands and the more tribal-minded, mystical races of the North. For recent centuries, perhaps the most fundamental expression of this came in the split of approach within the Church of Christ itself, the divergent paths taken by the mainly Protestant North and the basically Catholic South.

Their differences have found expression in many ways throughout the centuries, including, we would suggest, in the furniture styles that each has favored—as indeed is true in almost all the arts. It would be too simple to insist that all full-blown and heavily decorated styles were Catholic at root and from the South, or that all simple styles find their inspiration in the North. The purity of the Early Renaissance works would seem to refute this, though it is interesting to try and see just how far such a stylistic contention may be justified. One should not go too far with such a hypothesis, since so many other factors (from politics to climate, etc.) have played a part in these developments. As we shall see, for instance, royal tastes were markedly influential in the heyday of the monarchies. Certainly climate long dictated the most readily available materials, or did so till easy transport changed the situation. Thus, for centuries, walnut dominated in the South and oak in the North; and each encouraged, if they did not quite demand, certain technical approaches. Where exotic woods did occur, it was in small quantities that restricted their use to special pieces or for inlay or marquetry.

But there are other, often seemingly quite unimportant, factors of inheritance whose influence has been of the greatest significance. Unlike Orientals or many Africans, for instance, the European and his descendants elsewhere do not, as a matter of custom, squat as a natural seating posture. They sit, whether on a throne or on a rush-bottomed chair, a bench or a sofa. This is an expression of the Mediterranean upper-class tradition from ancient Egyptian and classical times. From this practice the most basic of our furniture—the seat—takes its form. From this also the height of our tables, whether static or trestle, is

determined. It may well be that the rather inconvenient height of early coffers arose from the fact that these were as often used for sitting as for storage. The *cassapanca* of the Italians or the box seat of the Tudors supports this idea. Beds, too, in general practice were raised, as distinct from many Eastern forms of sleeping custom which favor just an unrolled mat or cushions on the floor. Thus, quite simple everyday practices may have laid down the terms (i.e., suggested the form) for almost all our furniture today, since, apart from sleeping purposes, its fabrication started at root with man's need for something to sit *on*, something to sit or eat *at*, and something to store things *in* once he began to accumulate material possessions. It is a striking feature that, however elaborate and however purely decorative furnishings of later centuries became, they still at least pretended to serve one or another of these purposes. Indeed, among the hundreds of objects illustrated here, the only totally "phony" piece is Robert Adam's device for displaying some Italian marble plaques *(Plate 328)*—and even this is made to look like a kind of wall cabinet, though of little practical use.

If we have chosen to start our catalogue with the Renaissance in Italy, it is not because the great early medieval courts had no furnishings at all; but the number of such pieces was always relatively scant, and those which have come down to us are so very limited in number as to be almost without effect upon our aesthetic consciousness. This lack is quite logical and readily understood when one considers that medieval rulers traveled continuously by reason of their wars or regular forays to see that their subjects were kept in order. Moving about from castle to castle, they generally took with them on a baggage train all that might be required for use, or even as background panoply and decoration. This meant that their furniture had to be movable (hence the words *meuble* and *mobile*); folding seats, trestle tables that could be set away, tapestries that rolled up, convenient bedding, and a few cushions or pillows, together with utensils and table service, made up the bulk of their possessions. In general, it was only the churches and religious houses, as reasonably stable institutions, that had permanent fittings to any great extent. Medieval imagery and manuscript illuminations sometimes show apparently learned persons in some reasonably civilized setting, with a chair and desk of some recognizable design and with possibly a book or two on a carved shelf or cupboard, which might also serve to display some decorated vessel. We see similar luxuries in occasional representations of wealthier

10

burgher houses in towns, where communal protection led to some social security and a living standard that was not to be expected in the countryside.

Ecclesiastical domination and design is emphasized by the architectural styles of furnishings created for, and suited to, incorporation into the church buildings of the times. Other than such religious items as choir stalls or sacristy chests and wardrobes, which are not within our field of interest here, the number of unquestionable pieces of Early Gothic domestic furniture that have come down to us is limited indeed, though a host of 19th-century "reproductions," "restorations," "fakes," or whatever one may call them, do exist to tell the tale. Further explanation for this lack may lie in the fact that, especially in the North, not until the late 15th century could any fairly widespread sense of cultivated living be found.

Renaissance and Baroque in the South

For the above reasons, then, we have here regarded the broader lay movement as having opened in Italy, where it is pertinent to trace its background and development. The social and political situation that had evolved in the Italian Peninsula by Gothic times involved a number of autonomous states of varying size and character. Some of these were duchies and marquisates under traditional secular rulers, some were papal domains, and others such as Florence and Siena had developed into republics. Few were very extensive, but all shared one noteworthy feature—their focus on a fairly large and usually rather wealthy fortified city, which offered some haven from the eternal wars, providing the reasonably secure surroundings in which some level of culture could emerge. Such emergence of a cultivated life was generally supported and encouraged—though, as far as domestic furniture was concerned, this did not develop on any real scale until the 15th century even in the South. When the Renaissance did burst forth, about the second quarter of the 15th century, it came as a native manifestation and nearly a hundred years before it arose in the rest of Europe. The essentially Northern qualities of Gothic style had never been sympathetic to the Italians, and they abandoned its alien tenets as quickly as they could.

Against this background, somehow, in spite of endless interfamily, intercity, interstate, and even internationally provoked disputes, the money and time and effort were forthcoming to house God and the hierarchy of His Church, as well as the leaders of the state, with a luxury and taste that had not been seen for many centuries. Patronage was drawn from men whose instincts and conditioning found nothing contradictory between studying classical philosophy and engaging in battle, between commissioning or saving art and killing people. It was a remarkable time indeed. Each wealthy patron vied with the other to obtain the finest artists and the ablest craftsmen of the day, who in association with their cultivated sponsors were the people who shaped the evolution of this truly civilized advance.

In addition to creating paintings or sculpture, many of the artists of this era practiced architecture; thus the same man could very likely build a fortress or palace, decorate it with frescoes or carving, and supervise or execute the great ceilings, chimney breasts, and door surrounds which are so marked a feature of the day. In addition to all this accomplishment, none thought himself above designing plates and ewers, cabinets or *cassone*, or even coaches and sleds for his patrons. No wonder that, at least in the greater houses, the idea of furniture as part and parcel of an overall decorative scheme grew up and that pieces might be made as much for decoration as for practical use. This was to remain a feature of Italian furniture throughout. At the outset, in reaction to the pinnacles and crockets of Gothic style, the plain clean lines of the new architecture dominated the cupboards and chairs and tables as well as the new palaces. The style thus evolved was destined to last for generations, especially in the provinces, and has continued to enjoy no little vogue even in fairly recent times.

As the 15th century advanced, so did the classicizing intellectualism of the courts. When not too thoroughly engaged by war, these circles still continued the Maecenas traditions established by the previous generation. In this way, and despite the prevailing troubles, Italy remained the main aesthetic source and the chief inspiration for the whole Continent. Yet somehow the fire of Renaissance genius seemed to have died down. The clean simplicity of Early Renaissance Florence was soon to be replaced by ever-greater elaboration of form and detail and a more and more mannered handling of ornament. Indeed, simplicity as a desirable aesthetic feature was soon to be abandoned in Italy as far as furniture was concerned. The earlier paneled *cassone*, with their plain or simply painted fronts, gave way to monumental pieces that might be shaped and carved like an antique sarcophagus. Beds and seats became ever more enormous, to remain in keeping with the changed surroundings. Ornament became heavier and heavier until, as the 16th century progressed, the figures and motifs born of earlier, more integral classical adaptations seem merely banged on in many instances. If colored marbles or varicolored woods were applied, it was often more as an overloaded patterning in effect, rather than the sensitive creation of a work of art by means of such a medium. Mouldings of this period look merely lumpier or heavier, applied with the careless affluence to which a schoolchild might be prone upon finding too much whipped cream.

At the end of the 15th century and the opening of the 16th, there was a movement whereby the lead in cultural, as well as spiritual, affairs was eased away from Florence and the Northern courts and was focussed on the pope in Rome. If interstate and interfamily feuds were still sustained, it was usually because of some matter concerning the papacy. Obtaining this prize, now virtually an Italian monopoly, or at least influencing it, kept all and sundry happily engaged. The viciousness of the contests for St. Peter's throne and the maneuverings of the papacy are the keynote of this period. These machinations involved people like the Borgias, who though publicized more than most were little worse than many. They were ruthless in their demands, whether public or private, and in either field their call for grandeur encouraged high quality in art and furnishings. But, despite this auspicious start, Italy suffered like the rest of Europe in this era. Rome itself was sacked in 1527, and it took time and a further series of brilliant princes of the Church and papal successors to Julius II to set things aright once more.

By the end of the 16th century Italy—or at least the Roman-papal Italy—was ambitiously underway with reconstruction and refurbishment; a flaunting luxury and great magnificence took over from the fading sterility of court Mannerism as cardinals and popes set out to renovate "the greatest Church on earth," as well as to erect the greatest palaces to house the princes of the greatest Church on earth. Such worldliness in churchmen may now appear unChristian, but it certainly bred magnificence. Under their cultivated guidance new ideas and new breath came, and with these came new ideas for furniture. The style that evolved by the turn of the century is that which we call "baroque."

Baroque has sometimes been called "the art of the Counter Reformation." It did indeed serve that spiritual movement's aims, reflected its attitudes, and flourished where it triumphed. At the same time it is important to keep in mind that, as a style or taste, it

was a fairly normal reaction against the studied formality into which court Mannerism had fallen. Perhaps the most immediately apparent effect of baroque ideas on the interiors of the time was its uninhibited delight in the splendor of the settings as a whole. A baroque room does not invite you to examine it for intellectual content or to discourse upon such details as the erudite literary reference in this picture, the applied decoration of that cabinet, or the wall or ceiling panels, as did the more studied decorative work of the Mannerists. It absorbs—one might better say, overwhelms—the viewer in a sensuous pool of affluence and greatness. It is as turtle soup to gruel. While the basic ideas may not have been entirely revolutionary, the sumptuousness of the figure-strewn ceilings and covings, with their myriad swags and stuccoes, abundant painting and carving, or of the tapestries, frescoes, or colorful silks and damasks on the walls was on an unprecedented scale.

The actual furniture exhibited the same elements of the new style that influenced the sculpture of the period. If these elements derived from the studied intellectual poses of the decades that had gone before, they nevertheless were soon extended into the fantasies we have inherited. The endlessly flowing draperies, foliage, and figures which were so theatrical and splendid in the great sculptural altarpieces were now adapted and transmogrified in the carving of the legs and backs of chairs or supports for cabinets and tables, where, however spectacular or even functional, they can scarcely be said to make sober sense, when viewed with detached judgment. The gods and goddesses, nudes and gargoyles which peered from under every niche and moulding could be most effective in their proper setting. The exuberance that had gone into giving a literally solid magnificence to God on earth—in opposition to an attitude of puritan iconoclasm—served also to heighten the ambience of the richer of God's servants on earth. The larger the amount, the heavier and weightier the gold, the better. The softer the padding, the richer the silks, the more brilliant the damasks, the more appreciated they were. This was very much in keeping with the spirit which had been rebuilding St. Peter's in Rome on a grandiose scale.

Certainly Italy led in this development, and by the early 1600s had laid down the formulas which governed the new style, as far as anything would govern it at all. This inevitably meant that at its height it was a rich man's hobby—one for princes only, whether of church or state. For the rest of the populace, it could only provide ideas to be modified as far as their purses would allow. It also meant that its traits were likely to be fundamentally unsympathetic to Protestants, and hence to most Northerners. This is indeed what happened, and while some of its decorative influences may have penetrated elsewhere in details, the style at its full remained essentially a Southern and Catholic phenomenon.

Virtually, then, where Italy led, the rest of the Catholic Mediterranean followed. All the same, these influences were often retardataire and certainly persisted, outside the immediate court circles, for a long time. In this way, what were basically Renaissance or early baroque designs continued well into the 18th century in more conservative areas. By the same token, Gothic influences from the Spanish-dominated Low Countries made their impact especially at the outset, and Moorish techniques and influences persisted long after the Moors had left Spain. Such an "outpost" phenomenon was reasonable; and as our plates display, the combination of this heritage both in Spain and Portugal produced more or less easily recognizable local permutations and combinations of design. In some degree, southern France adhered to Italian tastes, just as the northern part persisted in a Northern Gothic tradition, in spite of developments in and around Paris. We shall touch on these last-mentioned in the second part of this introductory section, which deals with Renaissance and baroque tendencies in the North.

Renaissance and Baroque in the North

If we have started with Italy in the 15th century and moved right on through the 16th, it is because Italy was so far in advance of the war-torn North throughout this whole period that it was almost the only area to be taken seriously so far as furniture of any distinction is concerned and led the rest of the Continent. Apart from a few leading centers such as the great merchant ports and trading cities, little was produced of more than antiquarian interest in the Northern areas at this time. As in Italy, it needed the contacts, wealth, and security of a fortified city to enable such facets of culture to develop outside the sphere of ecclesiastical protection and patronage. Most feudal lords would have considered craftsmanship better spent on building fortresses or making armor. Thus it was mainly in the great towns that the sudden burst of civilized activity flourished in the decades around 1500.

If for Northern Europe the 16th century was later to be dominated by the Reformation and its austerity, the early years had opened with a blaze of still-Catholic personalities, culminating in the meeting of Francis I of France and Henry VIII of England at the Field of the Cloth of Gold, in a display of pomp that has remained to stagger history. Although it may have emphasized the now fairly undisputed power of kings as opposed to the whole feudal hierarchy, it was fundamentally a medieval pageant of feudal luxury. Its attitudes still play-acted the old ways, with kings and barons side by side in brave display—but for the last time. Typically, Henry then met with Emperor Charles V a few days later and a few miles away to sign a pact against his erstwhile friend, host, guest, or enemy. That same year (1520) Luther was excommunicated. The years to follow showed a different face indeed, as in the name of God—admittedly often but thinly cloaking dynastic ambition—a period of civil and international wars set in which lasted, on and off, for a century or more and buried the remains of chivalry. The graces fell before a puritan iconoclasm which, outside a few aristocratic circles, not only affected church carvings but also menaced the whole effort at an advance from near-barbarity. These were all matters of no little significance for our story.

If religion was in turmoil, all was not static in the political field, and at least the larger monarchies were on the rise. With this trend the whole social structure began to change, for government came to be administered from a permanent palace in a capital city rather than from some often makeshift, peripatetic headquarters. Reasonably enough, the great new palaces called for furnishings in keeping with the kingly state. This was not a totally new phenomenon, but the diffusion of court taste to a fairly numerous crowd of court favorites and hangers-on led to an increase in the demand for a higher standard of life. At the same time, the stability of a strong central government helped to promote more settled circumstances and so contributed to some advance in civilized amenities, for those who could afford them. If the monarchs took the lead, their most prominent subjects soon followed as best they might. It was from such circles that the idea of furniture as much for decoration as for use was furthered in the North. As in Italy, elaboration of this idea throughout the wealthier sections of the rest of Europe was the great contribution of the 16th century. Chairs and tables, coffers and buffets, were all loaded with Italian-type decoration so dear to the mannered princely courts. Pseudo-classical conceits such as masks and caryatids, sphinxlike inventions, and monstrous beasts were pressed into service to ornament the classically architectural pieces destined for the state rooms of the great of this era.

Nonetheless, it would be misleading to paint the picture of a 16th-century Northern European court too rosily. Apart from the very greatest, whose habitués had always had some tradition of cultivated existence, the mass of "cousins," peers, and nobles, as their portraits show, were liable to be a pretty brutish lot. They might be tough enough and could wield outrageous weapons, kill animals for hours on end, or campaign with the crudest of their soldiery, but further than this few cared to go. At best a little lechery or simple music extended their interests beyond hunting, warfare, or food and drink, where quantity or curiosity seems to have taken the place of quality. A few rulers and courtiers, such as Queen Elizabeth I of England, were literate, but many others could scarcely write their names. Almost all had political shrewdness, or they would have lost their places—and with this attribute came some sense of proper background and surroundings.

Here and there some vast half-palace, half-castle might be built which made some concession to being something other than a fortress, and even some manor houses of distinction rose. Nonetheless, the refinements of living and design that were to play so great a part for later generations were then scarcely thought of. Small wonder, then, that—with a few exceptions—the furniture of the time was often coarse and heavy, clumsy in design and frequently indifferent in execution. For most of the upper classes, as for others, furniture was still basically regarded as something for use, though certain pieces such as fine imported cabinets of ebony or marble inlay or intarsia work began to be transported or sent off as lavish gifts, to stand against the tapestries and lend an aura of decor, if not great distinction, to the halls and corridors of the noble and wealthy.

Apart from this growing influence from the central courts, there still remained the patronage of the burghers of the wealthy towns, most of whom had prospered somehow amid the confusion and strife of the times and had established not only some independence of rights and dues but also a way of life quite different from that at the courts. Between these and the fashionable aristocratic society, there might well be differences—and often some despite.

To the guildmasters of the cities with expanding enterprise, courtiers were little more than parasites and pimps and flatterers. Certainly for the 16th century, with which we are concerned, the burgess was often of considerable account and proud of his traditions and his town. While some sought patents of gentility, a large majority of the townsmen were quite content with their lot and quite deliberately kept their ways, and with them their demands, within their households, where tradition and conservatism flourished. Everywhere this middle class was likely to distrust new fashion and sought a background of more solid qualities that had the approval of precedent. It is largely their furnishings which have been preserved for us today—robust, clumsy, and showy stuff. At the same time, conservatism did not mean that these burghers were totally averse to some elaboration of decoration that might testify to their importance; indeed they liked it, and in the normal course, the heavier it was the better. This was especially noticeable in the plate and silverware they set out as witness to their station and prosperity. Even quite puritan persons were vulnerable on this score. The result of this social phenomenon was that until the 19th century there were likely to be two styles running concurrently in any area at any one time: namely, a court or more advanced fashion, with which we shall be chiefly concerned here; and a second style that was not necessarily an outmoded one but an approach adjusted to the tastes and requirements of the richer bourgeoisie just described.

But in the later 1500s, whosoever the patron might be, it was not easy for those few who wanted something more than sheer utility to find inspiration. Traditional Gothic—the natural art of the Northerners—had died out with the feudal society for which it had been purveyed. Puritanism was no help, and as a result the craftsmen were compelled to turn to Italy, usually through one of the books of ornament and design engraved (and thus translated) by a Frenchman or German or some other foreign draftsman.

The other main source, itself strongly influenced by Italian design, lay in the still-Catholic Low Countries. There, the new religion had quickly put a stop to the flourishing trade of the carving workshops, which had long exported altarpieces and devotional figures through the many waterways to which they had ready access. So, the carvers carried on as best they could with secular production. Richly carved cupboards, buffets, and panels and such, which soon found their way throughout the North, were to dominate the Northern styles well into the 17th and, in remoter parts, even the 18th century. If religion or need was pressing, craftsmen also emigrated, and names of artisans from hereabouts occur quite far afield. Most of the best such sculpture and carving

14

found in 16th-century England came from just such sources. Through these itinerant, often immigrant, Northern craftsmen the elegant masks and gargoyles of the Mannerists became the clumsy things we see on much of this work; and if, on occasion, some simple strapwork or carved foliage seems reasonably set out, it is but a small mercy to be thankful for.

In France, where there existed something of both worlds, a style of some respectability and elegance emerged, but this was evolved mainly at and for the aristocratic focus of the society. Here, there seemed to be some blend between the Catholic and Italian-slanted court, forging ahead with accomplished Italian artists and design, and the influence of another group, both within royal circles and among nobility from the provinces, who were certainly attracted to Reformation tenets. Though the problem was nominally settled by the St. Bartholomew's Massacre in 1572, the effects of this intermingling remained, seen both in architecture and in furniture. As a result, the Italian, classical architectural forms were modified by Gallic elegance, and—presumably in deference to trends current elsewhere—a blend of nicely turned austerity arose. As our illustrations show, these results were most agreeable, and this artistic restraint continued until superseded by the more extravagant influences that came with the establishment of Versailles.

If craftsmanship of some precision was maintained elsewhere in Europe, it was with the elaborate cabinets and coffers that came mainly from the traditional woodworking areas of southern Germany. Sometimes called "Nonesuch" work in English (in tribute to a palace of Henry VIII), these carvings show busy scenes of some charm and little art, but with a great deal of artifice and technical competence. Designed for a patron class whose aesthetic appreciation was limited, by their very ingenuity they contrived to offer a substitute more readily accepted by their patrons. For decades these works were much sought after and were often sent around as imposing gifts by the rich. The ebony cabinets with painted drawers which came from France and Flanders a little later also performed just such a service, and with slightly better taste.

Elsewhere in German-speaking lands, a more enlightened or advanced court might lead the way toward newer things, whereas in the provinces a very set traditional design was most likely to prevail. In such remote areas as northernmost Germany, cupboards and coffers dating from the 18th century are still Late Gothic in design. As was seen, Spain followed more or less the same pattern of taste and styles: Italian influence prevailing at the intensely Catholic court, with an extended persistence of older traditions—even Mudéjar—outside the main centers.

1 Oak bench and draw-leaf table.
   English, first half of 16th century.
   Victoria and Albert Museum, London.

2 Oak buffet with Gothic carved
   panels and details. North Holland,
   first quarter of 16th century.
   Rijksmuseum, Amsterdam.

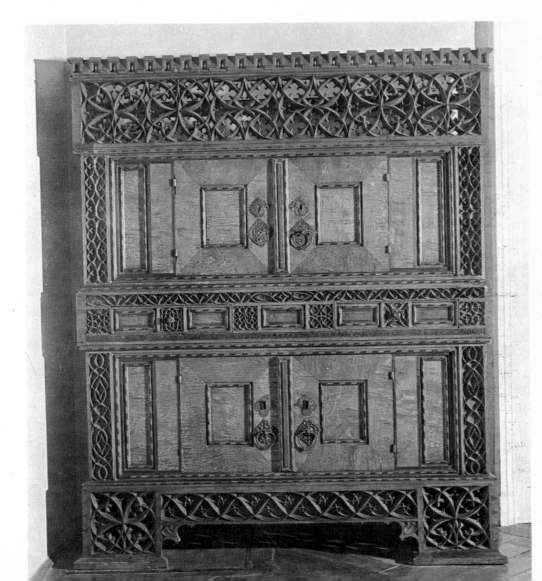

3 Canopy bed with incised decoration.
German (Upper Rhine), early 16th century.
Historisches Museum, Basel.

4 Walnut hall chair. Italian (Florentine), 16th
century. Museo Bardini, Florence.

18

5 Walnut *cassapanca* (chest, here fitted with arms and back to serve for seating). Italian (Tuscan), 16th century. Palazzo Davanzati, Florence.

6 Walnut cupboard (*credenza*). Italian (Tuscan). 16th century. Horne Museum, Florence.

7 Walnut cupboard. Italian (Tuscan), 16th century. Museo Bardini, Florence.

9   Carved walnut table with trestle support.
    Italian (Tuscan), mid-16th century. Palazzo
    Davanzati, Florence.

10 Stool with carved relief in Mannerist style
    and painted decoration. Italian (Tuscan),
    second half of 16th century. Museo Bardini,
    Florence.

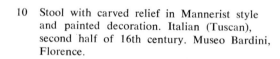

8   Carved walnut candlestick. Italian (Tuscan),
    16th century. Museo Bardini, Florence.

11 Walnut table on carved triangular base, with hexagonal top containing drawers. Italian (Florentine), 16th century. Private collection, Florence.

12 Walnut coffer with high-relief scenes of Hercules, partly gilt. Italian (Tuscan), 16th century. (Sphinx feet may be of later date.) Palazzo Reale, Turin.

13 *(above left)* Two-part carved walnut cupboard, inset with marble panels. French, c. 1550. Musée des Arts Décoratifs, Paris.

14 *(left)* Walnut panel carved with allegory of Virtues. French (School of Fontainebleau), mid-16th century. Italian Mannerist influences introduced into France are apparent in this carving related to Fontainebleau stuccowork.

16 Walnut episcopal chair with marble inset panels. French, c. 1560. Louvre, Paris (formerly property of bishops of Vienne).

15 *(above)* Ballroom at Fontainebleau (Gallery of Henry II). French, 1540–50. Built by the architect Philibert de l'Orme, this imposing chamber has frescoes by Primaticcio; its splendid coffered ceiling, designed by De l'Orme, was executed by the noted Italian woodcarver Scibec de Carpi.

17 Carved walnut buffet with marble insets. French, c. 1570. Victoria and Albert Museum, London.

18 Carved walnut cupboard in two sections. French (from Jujurieux, near Lyons). The original lining inside bears the date 1591. Rijksmuseum, Amsterdam.

19 Oak "conversation chair." French,
mid-16th century. Musée des Arts
Décoratifs, Paris.

20 Walnut cabinet. French, second half of 16th
century. This columned piece stresses simple
architectonic lines rather than applied
decoration. Musée des Arts Décoratifs, Paris.

21 Walnut "conversation chair" with architectonic
carved back and scroll cresting. French,
third quarter of 16th century. Louvre, Paris.

23 *(right)* Walnut secretary-cabinet, with architectonic front inlaid with different woods and semiprecious stones. Italian (Lombardy), made at Como and dated 1613. Museo del Castello, Milan.

22 *(above)* Cabinet veneered in ebony, with relief panels showing scenes from the life of the Virgin. French (attributed to Jean Macé of Blois), first half of 17th century. Besides its carved panels, this cabinet is notable for its elegant balustrade, classical figurines, and graceful serpentine supports. Musée des Arts Décoratifs, Paris.

24 *(right)* Walnut wardrobe. Spanish, early 17th century. This simple-lined piece has finely carved panels of varied sizes, symmetrically arranged, on its front. Museo de Artes Decorativas, Madrid.

25 Colbert Room from Villacerf. French,
Louis XIII style, c. 1640. The paneled walls
and ceiling are painted with classical motifs on
a cream-colored ground. Musée Carnavalet,
Paris.

26 Carved walnut wardrobe with veneer panels of
burr walnut. Italian (Venetian), c. 1600.
Designed by the sculptor-architect Jacopo
Sansovino, this sculpture-decorated piece was
formerly in the Villa Garzoni at Ponte Casale.
Cini Collection, Venice.

27 *(below)* Walnut chest of drawers, with inset
spiral columns at corners. Italian (Parma),
mid-17th century. Marchi Collection, Castello
di Montechiarugolo.

28

28 *(above)* Chest of drawers with carved walnut
mouldings, drawer pulls, corner figures, and
lion feet. Italian (Genoa), early 17th century.
Acton Collection, Florence.

29 *(right)* Carved walnut secretary, with
burr-walnut veneer. Italian (Liguria), early
17th century. The exhuberant carving includes
figures of Adam, Eve, Hercules, David, and
hippocamps. Museo del Castello, Milan.

31 *(right)* Ebony cabinet with finely carved panels of various rare woods. Bohemian (made at Eger), second quarter of 17th century. Museum für Kunsthandwerk, Frankfurt.

30 Cabinet with intarsia of rare woods, showing battle scenes and emblems. South German, 16th century (the stand is later). Victoria and Albert Museum, London.

32 *(right)* Cabinet with fall-front writing table, decorated with intarsia in rare woods (some tinted). German, bears monogram "HS" and the date 1560. Victoria and Albert Museum, London.

33 *(above)* Buffet inlaid with strapwork patterns in various woods. German (Cologne), dated 1583. Rijksmuseum, Amsterdam.

34 Two-section cupboard with architectonic front in Late Renaissance style. German (probably Augsburg), second half of 16th century. The architectural arrangement of the front resembles a two-story classical facade adorned with columns, pilasters, portals, and pediments of varied orders. Cini Collection, Castello di Monselice.

35 *(left)* Oak table with circular folding top and gate-leg. English, early 17th century. Victoria and Albert Museum, London.

36 *(below)* Walnut daybed with plain rails and carved head. English, late 17th century. Victoria and Albert Museum, London.

37 State Room from Old House, Bromley-by-Bow,
London. English, early 17th century. The oak
paneling is dated 1606. The carved oak
furniture includes the imposing bed, an inlaid
buffet, a draw-leaf table, chairs, and stools,
all typical of the period. Victoria and Albert
Museum, London.

39 *(above)* Oak armchair with contemporary cover of Turkey work. English (Warwickshire), c. 1660. Victoria and Albert Museum, London.

40 *(below)* Gate-leg table with oak top and turned legs. English, c. 1660. Victoria and Albert Museum, London.

38 Chair of carved, and originally painted, oak. English, c. 1635. Probably designed by Francis Cleyn, this chair was once in Holland House, London. Victoria and Albert Museum, London.

41 Pine traveling trunk, covered with leather decorated in nailwork. English, late 17th century. Victoria and Albert Museum, London.

42 Oak cupboard, its front mounted with ebony and inlaid with chestnut, ivory, and mother-of-pearl. English, dated 1653. This heavy, symmetrically paneled and decorated cabinet shows similarities to models from North Holland. Victoria and Albert Museum, London.

45 *(above)* Ferry house kitchen at Van Cortlandt
Manor, Croton-on-Hudson, New York. Colonial
American. Supervised by Sleepy Hollow
Restorations, this colonial interior makes use
of 17th-century country furniture.
(Photo: Louis H. Frohman)

43 *(top left)* Kitchen at Leffingwell Inn, Norwich,
Connecticut. Colonial American, built 1675.
This late-17th-century interior features early
country pieces. (Photo: Louis H. Frohman)

44 *(left)* Kitchen at Hempstead House, New
London, Connecticut. Colonial American, built
1678. The room is furnished with simple early
furniture and accessories, including a large
storage cupboard with butterfly hinges, carver
chairs, early Connecticut tables, and a rare
17th-century cradle. Herbs drying over the
fireplace are hung on original wooden herb
pole supported by wrought-iron herb hooks.
(Photo: Louis H. Frohman)

46 Joshua's Hall or keeping room, Hempstead House, New London, Connecticut. Colonial American, 1678.

47 (opposite) Hall and sleeping chamber, Buttolph-Williams House, Wethersfield, Connecticut. Colonial American, 1692.

48 (right) Sitting-bedroom from Hart House, Ipswich, Massachusetts. Colonial American; built c. 1670. With the exception of the late-17th-century gate-leg table from Pennsylvania, all the furniture in this room is of New England origin. The most important piece is the oak court cupboard; bearing the date 1684, it is attributed to Thomas Dennis, master joiner of Ipswich. Henry Francis du Pont Winterthur Museum, Wilmington, Delaware.

49 Folding chair (*sillón de caderas*), inlaid with ivory and wood mosaic in Moorish style (Mudéjar); seat and backrest of leather. Spanish, c. 1600. Museo de Santa Cruz, Toledo.

50 Wardrobe cabinet inlaid with ivory and various stained woods in Moorish style (Mudéjar). Spanish, c. 1600. Museo de Artes Decorativas, Barcelona.

51 Bed of turned wood, with headboard almost entirely covered in brasswork. Spanish (Salamanca), also showing Portuguese influence, second half of 17th century. The adjacent chair and *vargueño* cabinet are contemporary. Museo de Artes Decorativas, Madrid.

52 Canopy bed of exotic wood (mountings of gilded wood and metal). Spanish, late 16th century. Museo de Artes Decorativas, Madrid.

53 Carved walnut armchair, decorated with perforated "knotted cord" motif. Italian (Venetian), late 16th century. Casa Bagatti-Valsecchi, Milan.

54 Carved walnut canopy bed. Italian (Lombardy),
late 16th century. (Cartouche with Visconti
family arms added later.) Castello di
Somma Lombardo.

55 Room in Rosenborg Castle, Copenhagen.
Danish, second quarter of 17th century.
The carved wooden chairs flanking the
fireplace were made in 1718 by Johan Weys;
their tapestry covers are of slightly later date.
The silver firescreen is German (Augsburg),
datable about 1720.

56 *(above)* Fireplace in Rosenborg Castle, Copenhagen. Danish, 17th century. The pair of small silver tables were made by I. H. de Moor, about 1690, to stand at either side of the fireplace. The silver andirons, by an unknown craftsman, are of the same period.

57 *(right)* Carved and gilded candlestick, by Burchardt Precht, a German carver working in Stockholm during the late 17th century. Nordiska Museum, Stockholm.

58 *(below)* Ebony prie-dieu, lavishly inset with rare marbles and *pietre dure* panels depicting the Baptism of Christ and floral motifs. Italian (Florentine); bearing the device of Grand Duke Cosimo II of Florence, probably datable 1621. Palazzo Pitti, Florence.

59 *(above)* Carved wooden cabinet with polychrome inlay. German (Augsburg), begun in 1624 by Philipp Hainhofer, acquired in 1628 by Archduke Leopold of Austria and later given to Grand Duke Ferdinand II of Tuscany. Palazzo Pitti, Florence.

60 *(right)* Cabinet veneered in ebony, with drawer-fronts inlaid with other woods and ivory. (Carved figural base of gilded and painted wood was perhaps added later.) Italian, 1667, made in Florence by the Flemish cabinetmaker Leonardo van der Vim. Palazzo Pitti, Florence.

61 Salon de Guerre, Palace of Versailles.
French, 1678–84; designed by Charles Le Brun.
Stucco relief by Antoine Coysevox shows
Louis XIV crossing the Rhine.

Versailles and the Court Style

The illustrations in this section trace the elaborate court style which, starting with the foundation of Versailles, lasted for over a century both in France and in other areas under her influence.

    The example of the Salon de Guerre at Versailles (Plate 61) shows how the pervasive French classical restraint modified the Italian innovations, just as it had done in the previous century. We have only to compare the illustrations on the final pages of the first section with the opening selections here to see how this applies not only to the architectural whole but also to individual pieces.

    This is certainly reflected in "Boulle" furniture—that essentially French court development which lasted in favor for so long (pp. 57–61). The elaboration and yet delicate refinement of metal marquetry set in rich tortoise shell, together with bold but superbly worked gilt mounts, set a model of princely taste that survived for many decades. The rich floral marquetry (p. 56) and more exotic pieces (Plates 84, 87) represent an international taste. Such examples as these last might often be executed by craftsmen from the Low Countries working abroad.

    Whatever modifications of fashion may have appeared, this basically formal tradition dominated Régence pieces and also many of those which followed (pp.64–69). Without this established court style, a commode like that by Melchior Kambli (Plate 106) would never have been made for a patron of rococo such as Frederick the Great nearly a century later. Nor indeed would the regular type of what most people look upon as "French" furniture (pp. 72–81) ever have filled the halls and salons of the very rich up to our own times. Thus, although the more luxurious metal and tortoise shell of Boulle was replaced by parquetry and marquetry in wood, the formal court spirit persisted.

    Certain lines and patterns might change with the years, but the expression of absolutist pomp and circumstance remained firmly embedded as the taste of those in a more conservative tradition. If the exquisitely frivolous, feminine developments of rococo owe much to the inspiration of a group of French artists, other royal pieces bear witness to how long the Versailles taste persisted (pp. 79, 81), before their stylistic revival once more in the 19th century.

So important was the establishment of Versailles and the ideas of its creator Louis XIV for the whole European development of grand living that we have treated it as a separate section: "Versailles and the Court Style." A brief review of this, together with another on the opposing movement we have termed "The Protestant North," would seem to indicate the two main roots to which most later manifestations in the 18th century go back. Admittedly the emphasis is arbitrary since other influences, of course, came in; but we feel there is sufficient basis for taking this as something of a broad approach. At worst, it may merely be regarded for what it certainly is—an interesting point of departure.

While Italy could build and baroque could flourish in the first half of the 17th century, the Northern countries of Europe were not nearly so fortunate. Everywhere there was trouble and war. Over the central mainland, what is often termed the Thirty Years' War—one of the most confused and appalling conflicts the Continent had ever known—was likely to afford a battlefield and massacre at any moment, anywhere. France had religious and political disturbances as well. England merely had a revolution. No wonder these years were artistically among the least rewarding. Equally, no wonder that a sequence of events which helped to modify, if not to end, these things in the middle decades of the 17th century was deeply significant for European social history. The year 1648 saw the Treaty of Westphalia, which brought some peace; 1660 witnessed the restoration of the monarchy in England, and the latter years of that decade brought a factor of even greater significance for civilization and for the monarchy everywhere—the foundation of Versailles. This meant not only the building of one of the greatest and finest palaces the world had ever seen but also the statement of a political design which was to ensure the absolutism of monarchy for a century and more. It also revolutionized ideas on furniture.

Created not so much to house the king and his family or even the offices of government, Versailles was designed to be the hub and universe of France and the French nobility. In its vast area, all the latter who could afford it were assembled round the royal presence, which meant—and meant deliberately—that they were under royal surveillance. Families of the greatest rank and wealth who had before been sources of revolt and civil war were quickly brought to heel and kept in daily and obsequious vassalage in waiting upon the king. The process of demoralization—if it can be called such—was very quick, and by the second generation was complete. Virtually no one of great family or rank thought higher than to die for his king in war (if such was his line of endeavor) or of committing any baseness to obtain an invitation to some more exclusive private party in the king's company. Both means served to enhance such wealth and honor as they had, or to give them some if they had started with none.

To create the atmosphere in which such a move could be effective meant the creation, within the court, of a luxury and magnificence which would dazzle and overwhelm this world. Nothing but the finest and the most magnificent would do. At the same time, too effusive a display—as in Roman baroque—was not exactly what this king required. Control and, above all, dignity and manners were innate in Louis XIV, as indeed firmly within the French tradition.

The result evolved an approach to the furniture and furnishings which we have termed the court style, since in starting at Versailles it influenced for very many years not only France but all those princes who adopted the French taste or who sought to emulate this most successful political experiment and give their leading subjects bread and circuses in magnificent surroundings to keep them in their place.

In the new furniture, as in the architecture, an inherited classical restraint is manifest, despite the adoption of so many innovations from Italian baroque. The work of the Boulle family—which was to become so marked a feature of the time and last right through until World War I—seems to epitomize the compromise, in which the swirling baroque decorative forms that may appear in the running marquetry of tortoise shell and metal are kept within a volume that is classically severe, or would be so if the richness of the decoration were removed. Looked at in silhouette, they might have come from the 16th-century designer Jacques du Cerceau. But more exactly what occurred, as well as the range of it, is better shown in illustrations than in words.

There was one other issue in this court development that was to make an interesting mark on furniture development. Court etiquettes had always existed, and kings had used them to preserve the aura of apartness that their state required. With the sudden concentration on the court as focus of the nation, it was only natural that there should be reemphasis of such a principle. By the time Louis was well in the saddle, almost every move of king and courtiers when on parade was regulated by some ceremonial routine. Some of these were intimately bound up with furniture, and some objects took on certain features as a result. As formalities at court spread down through the social hierarchy, in increasingly modest form, this naturally extended the efforts.

From long tradition the court's day started with the levee, when the king made his formal rising. The ceremony, like the coucher at the end of the day when His Majesty returned to bed, was attended by the very highest in the land. Such a formal issue naturally called for splendid beds in splendid settings, though beds had long been a focal point of domestic life, especially as the habit grew for women to receive in bed. As the ritual extended, so the beds became more splendid still, and as the princes' subjects down the line sought to imitate their masters, so did the design of beds—at least among the very rich—tend to become ever more extravagant. A "state bed" became essential to any house of great pretension.

Similarly, toilet tables at which a part of all this intricate ceremony of the levee took place became very elaborate and dressed with every accoutrement of luxury, such as gold or silver mirrors, mounted brushes, combs, and other requisites. Again, down the line, great men would receive while being patched and powdered, and women of the aristocracy as well. Thus all the elaborate types of dressing tables evolved first for the leaders and then, in similar form, for their more ordinary subjects. To some extent, this ruler-to-subjects progression had always existed, but now the custom was amplified.

Court seating, in particular, was fraught with regulations. Normally only the king and queen might sit in the presence of courtiers, and then on thrones with armrests and backs. Sometimes special princes might have backs and arms on their chairs if they were honored with an invitation to be seated before ruling monarchs. Royal children had backs on their seats, but no armrests. Anyone else, if accorded such an honor—a cardinal, for instance, or sometimes duchesses—might sit, but only on a stool without back or arms. At different courts the details might be changed, but everywhere the basic principle remained. The sets of dining chairs we use today in which only one or two usually have armrests, stem from such autocratic tradition. The master of the house (as king) and the mistress (as queen) have those with armrests; the others at table, like the younger princes of the courts, must do without. While it would be unwise to overstress the influence of such social practices on every detail of design, they did exist and were of significant influence.

Naturally it took some little time for the impact of Versailles to spread as widely as it did. For one thing, many—even some of the greatest rulers of the epoch— needed time to gather funds for such a costly pastime. For another, the idea itself demanded something of a change in attitude both on the part of rulers and their subjects. By the 18th century a lot of imitators were on their way, however, and by its second decade a great spate of building, as well as furnishing, was going on especially in Catholic lands, for it was not only secular lords who might indulge themselves, but also a host of princes of the Church who followed in their way with full enthusiasm—and quite often with the greatest taste. Some remained faithful to Italian types; but outside Italy, many slavishly followed French models right on through the century, or at least until the Revolution. Others took the French ini-

tiative and blended it with brighter colors of their own, thereby providing the basis for the burst of rococo that ensued in German lands.

In this and in subsequent autocratic eras, it would be very interesting to know exactly how far and how many of these developments were due to direct intervention by a particular monarch. While these rulers may not have drawn the plans or made designs themselves, some of them certainly saw and chose the foremost artists they employed to execute their commissions. Whereas George I of Hanover and England may have been little interested in such artistic doings, Max Emanuel, the magic-working Elector of Bavaria, was an intensely personal patron, busying himself in studios and with his works of art even when in exile for a year or two. He personally sent his brilliant Flemish dwarf François Cuvilliés to Paris to be taught. The decorative results on the latter's return to Munich were prodigiously successful. The Schönborn bishops saw to it that they had everything of the finest. Ceilings by Tiepolo did not materialize unless the prince-bishop had personally selected such a great artist. Frederick the Great was in continual correspondence with his friend and architect Von Knobbelsdorf, who designed furnishings for Sans Souci. Not even military campaigns were allowed to interrupt his flow of questions about how new things might be made. His case is also interesting for the reverse of the medal it can show. Frederick did not appreciate native talents, least of all in literature. In his territories German taste and artistry did not flourish, though the French styles did. His sister, certainly, would intervene at Bayreuth, sometimes with most undesirable effect, such as when some family-worked pastels were imposed upon the walls.

Louis XV may not always have shown so open a concern in these matters of taste as his grandfather did; but at least one of his mistresses, the celebrated Madame de Pompadour, and her brother were directly influential in establishing fashion. Further, had the ruler not liked their efforts, these would assuredly have been eliminated.

The sum of all the evidence would suggest that direct intervention was likely to be the rule more often than the exception. Such practical aesthetic issues, at the time, were not regarded as outside the province of men—or even of gentlemen or princes. Architecture was indeed an estimable and encouraged occupation, and 18th-century architecture cannot be divorced from its interiors and decoration and, in consequence, from its furniture—all of which played such a significant part in creating a proper background for the court.

51

62 Gallery in Hôtel Lambert, Paris.
French, 1650–60. Built at the beginning of the
reign of Louis XIV, this sumptuous hall was
designed by Louis Le Vau. Charles Le Brun
painted its ceiling frescoes, and Rousseau did
the landscape panels on the walls.

63 Salon d'Apollon, Palace of Versailles.
French, 1671–81; designed by Charles Le Brun.
The painted ceiling shows the story of Apollo,
who symbolized Louis XIV. The gilded and
tapestried walls testify to the ornate taste
characteristic of that monarch's reign.

64 Carved and gilded wooden table, with figured marble top (one of a pair originally belonging to the Duc d'Antin). French, late 17th century. The monogram bears the initials of Louis XIV and his queen, Maria Teresa, who died in 1683. Palace of Versailles.

65 Carved and gilded wooden armchair, covered in silk damask. French, c. 1680; designed in the court style of J. Lepautre. Musée des Arts Décoratifs, Paris.

66 Writing table (so-called *bureau Mazarin*), with floral marquetry of wood and ivory. French, late 17th century. Victoria and Albert Museum, London (formerly at Château de Montargis).

67 *(above)* Chest of drawers, with floral marquetry of wood and ivory and with ormolu mounts. French, late 17th century. Victoria and Albert Museum, London (formerly at Château de Montargis).

68 *(left)* Two-section cabinet, with floral marquetry of wood and ivory. French, late 17th century. Victoria and Albert Museum, London (formerly at Château de Montargis).

69 (above) Wing chair with scrolled walnut legs
and stretchers. French, late 17th century.
The upper part is covered in *petit-point* of
naturalistic flowers on a black ground.
Musée des Arts Décoratifs, Paris.

70 (right) Wardrobe of ebony casework, with
Boulle floral marquetry panels and ormolu
mounts (one of a pair). French, late 17th
century; made by André-Charles Boulle.
Louvre, Paris.

71 (below left) Torchère of carved and gilded
wood. French, Louis XIV period, c. 1670.
Musée des Arts Décoratifs, Paris.

72 (below right) Casket of Boulle marquetry
over tortoise shell base, with ormolu mounts.
French, late 17th century. López-Willshaw
Collection, Paris.

73 Marriage chest with Boulle
marquetry decoration. French,
c. 1700; by an imitator or
assistant of Boulle. Wallace
Collection, London.

74 (right) Cabinet on stand, with
ebony veneer, Boulle marquetry,
and ormolu mounts. French, late
17th–early 18th century;
attributed to André-Charles Boulle.
Louvre, Paris (cliché des Musées
Nationaux).

75 Commode in Boulle style.
French, late 18th century; by
Étienne Levasseur. This piece
shows the revival of Boulle
marquetry during the Neoclassic
period. Palace of Versailles.

76 Commode (one of a pair). French, 1708–09; made by André-Charles Boulle for the Trianon. The marquetry is of brass and tortoise shell, and the mounts are ormolu. Palace of Versailles.

77 *(below and right)* Two drawings, designs for a torchère and for a dwarf cabinet. French, c. 1680; both attributed to André-Charles Boulle. Musée des Arts Décoratifs, Paris.

79 *(above)* Gilt-bronze bracket clock and bracket, decorated with Boulle marquetry and ormolu mounts. French, early 18th century. The movement is signed "Bastien à Paris." Victoria and Albert Museum, London.

78 *(above)* Clock decorated with Boulle marquetry of metal inlaid on tortoise shell base. French, c. 1700. The ormolu figures represent Cupid triumphing over Time. Wallace Collection, London.

80 Ebony veneer commode in Boulle style, with *contre-partie* brass and tortoise shell marquetry. French, early 18th century. The decorative patterns show the influence of Jean Bérain. Wallace Collection, London.

81 *(above)* Mirror with a frame of Boulle marquetry and with ormolu mounts and candle brackets. French, early 18th century; possibly by André-Charles Boulle. Wallace Collection, London.

82 *(top right)* Writing table with Boulle marquetry and ormolu mounts. French, c. 1715; made by André-Charles Boulle for Max Emanuel, Elector of Bavaria. Louvre, Paris.

83 *(right)* Writing table with Boulle marquetry, raised on scrolled legs. French, c. 1700. Decorative motifs include arabesques and dancing figures. Bayerisches Nationalmuseum, Munich.

84–85 *(right and below left)* Large cabinet of
ebony and other exotic woods. French, late 17th
century. The ornaments are of gilt bronze
(ormolu), and the door is set with *pietre dure*
(see detail). This piece was delivered to the
French royal collection in 1683. Collection of
Duke of Northumberland, Alnwick Castle,
England.

86 Carved and gilded wooden daybed (headboard
cresting is missing). French, second half of
17th century. Musée des Arts Décoratifs, Paris.

87 Cabinet of red tortoise shell, with marquetry of brass and pewter (*première-partie*) showing battle scenes. (Stand and cresting are partly of carved and gilded wood.) French, c. 1700. The style here seems to show influence from Germany or the Low Countries. The piece was given by Louis XIV to his grandson the Duc d'Anjou (who became Philip V of Spain) in 1700. Private collection, Paris.

88 Torchère of carved and gilded wood. French, Louis XIV style, c. 1690. Musée des Arts Décoratifs, Paris.

89 *(above)* Writing table with marquetry of gilt brass, pewter, and ebony and with gilt-bronze mounts. French, c. 1700. The design falls between the so-called *bureau Mazarin* and the 18th-century *bureau plat*. Collection of Baron de Rédé, Paris.

90 *(left)* Armchair with scrolled frame of carved and gilded wood. French, late 17th century. Musée des Arts Décoratifs, Paris.

91 *(above)* Design for a carved paneled
door. French, early 18th century;
by Daniel Marot (c. 1663–1752), a
pupil of Boulle who carried his style
to Holland and England. Musée des
Arts Décoratifs, Paris.

92 *(right)* Carved wooden door, painted and
gilded, leading to the chapel in the Palace of
Versailles. French, c. 1685–90.

93 (above) Carved and gilded wooden armchair.
French, c. 1720. Collection of Baron de Rédé,
Paris.

94 *(left)* Wooden console bracket, finely carved with classical details. French, early Louis XIV period, mid-17th century. (The japanned metal urn is of later date.) Musée des Arts Décoratifs, Paris.

95 *(right)* Carved walnut armchair, covered in contemporary floral needlework on black ground. French, c. 1720. Musée des Arts Décoratifs, Paris.

96 *(below)* Bed of carved and gilded wood. French, later Louis XIV period, end of 17th century. Musée des Arts Décoratifs, Paris (formerly belonged to Rohan family).

97 (left) Cabinet of Japanese lacquer, supported on gilt-wood stand. French, late 17th century. Bibliothèque de l'Arsenal, Paris.

98 (below) Side table of carved and gilded wood, with marble top. French, early 18th century; in the style of Oppenord. Musée des Arts Décoratifs, Paris (formerly at Château de Chenonceau).

100 Side table of carved and gilded wood. French, c. 1737; by Claude Roumier. Palace of Versailles.

101 Console table of carved and gilded wood, with marble top. French, c. 1745. *Cabinet doré* of Madame Adelaide, Palace of Versailles.

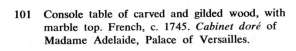

99 Side chair of natural wood. French, early 18th century. Musée des Arts Décoratifs, Paris.

102 (above) Side table of carved and gilded wood, with marble top. Italian (Genoa), c. 1700. Palazzo Reale, Genoa.

103 Armchair of carved and gilded wood. Italian (Piedmont, but closely following Louis XIV style), c. 1700 (petit-point cover of slightly later date). Palazzo Reale, Turin.

104 Console table of carved and gilded wood, with marble top. Italian, mid-18th century; bears the monogram of Carlo Emanuele III (1730–73). Palazzo Reale, Turin.

105 Bedroom of the Duke of Genoa. Italian,
mid-18th century. Palazzo Reale, Genoa.

106 *(above)* Commode veneered in tortoise shell, with ormolu decoration and top of lapis lazuli and silver. German, c. 1760; by Johann Melchior Kambli, cabinetmaker to Frederick the Great. Neues Palais, Potsdam. (Photo: Rudolf Ulmer, by courtesy of Kohler & Amelang, Berlin)

108 *(left)* Astronomical clock. French, mid-18th century; ormolu casework designed by C. S. Passemant, with bronzes signed by Jacques Caffieri. Presented to the Academy of Sciences in 1749, this splendid example of High Rococo craftsmanship was given to King Louis XV a few years later. Palace of Versailles.

109 *(below)* Paneling of carved and gilded wood, Cabinet de la Pendule, Palace of Versailles. French, 1738–39; by J. Verberckt.

107 *(left)* Writing table *(bureau plat)*, veneered with kingwood and with legs and mounts of ormolu. French, c. 1735; not signed, but ormolu attributed to Jacques Caffieri. Made for the Duc de Choiseul, it is said to have belonged later to Talleyrand and Metternich. Private collection.

110 (above) Astronomical clock with works by
Antoine Morand. French, early 18th century.
The monumental case is veneered with
kingwood, with ormolu mounts in 17th-century
style. The clock was given to Louis XIV in
1706. Palace of Versailles.

111 (above) Dwarf wardrobe veneered with
kingwood, with ormolu mounts. French,
c. 1715. Bibliothèque Mazarine, Paris.

112 (right) Commode covered in
kingwood parquetry, with leaf
and mask mounts of ormolu.
French, c. 1715–20; attributed
to André-Charles Boulle.
Louvre, Paris (cliché des
Musées Nationaux).

113 *(right) Commode en tombeau*, with kingwood
veneer and ormolu mounts. French, c. 1720–30.
Musée Jacquemart-André, Paris.

114 *(below)* Commode with kingwood veneer and
ormolu mounts. French, late 18th century(?).
The style is of the Régence period, but the
piece is stamped *"J. C. Saunier"* and may have
been made later. Victoria and Albert Museum,
London.

115 Commode with kingwood and satinwood
     veneer and ormolu mounts. French, 1739;
     made by Antoine Gaudreaux for the king's
     chamber at Versailles. The gilt mounts are by
     Jacques Caffieri. Wallace Collection, London.

116 *(left)* Wardrobe with kingwood and tulipwood
     veneer and ormolu mounts. French, c. 1725–30;
     by Charles Cressent. Musée des Arts
     Décoratifs, Paris.

117 *(above)* Game table with rosewood and
     kingwood veneer and removable playing
     surface. French, first half of 18th century; by
     Jacques Dubois (1693–1763). Private
     collection, Paris.

118 *(above)* Writing table *(bureau plat)*, with kingwood veneer and ormolu mounts. French, first half of 18th century; attributed to Antoine Gaudreaux. This piece was at Versailles in 1740. Ministry of Finance, Paris.

119 *(below)* Commode with kingwood veneer and ormolu mounts. French, second quarter of 18th century; by Charles Cressent. Here the nearly full-round gilt corner mounts attain the lineaments and importance of individual sculpture. Residenzmuseum, Munich.

120 *(above)* *Secrétaire à capucin* (or *à la Bourgogne*), with veneer and inlay of various woods. French, late 18th century; by Roger Vandercruse (Lacroix; 1728–99). Musée Nissim de Camondo, Paris.

121 Commode with kingwood and tulipwood
veneer, ormolu mounts, and marble top.
French, c. 1745–50; by Charles Cressent.
Louvre, Paris.

122 *(above)* Writing table *(bureau plat)*, with tulipwood and kingwood veneer and ormolu mounts. French, c. 1730; by Charles Cressent. Louvre, Paris.

123 *(below)* Medal cabinet in commode form, with kingwood veneer, ormolu mounts (by the brothers Slodtz), and marble top. French, 1738; made by Antoine Gaudreaux for King Louis XV. Palace of Versailles.

124 *(below)* Corner cupboard *(encoignure)* with kingwood veneer. French, 1755; made by Gilles Joubert for Louis XV. This piece was ordered to match the ruler's medal cabinet *(123)*, designed nearly a decade earlier by Gaudreaux. Palace of Versailles.

125 *(below)* Two-drawer commode, with lacquer panels, ormolu mounts, and marble top. French, late 18th century; by Nicolas **Petit** (1732–91). Palace of Versailles.

126 Cylinder writing table, with mahogany veneer and ormolu mounts. French, late 18th century. A more or less identical piece is found at Charlottenburg; this one was probably given by Louis XVI to Catherine the Great of Russia. Louvre, Paris (cliché des Musées Nationaux).

127 Veneered commode with gilt appliqué mounts. Danish, 1740–43; made by C. J. Preisler. Rosenborg Castle, Copenhagen.

128 *(above)* Veneered commode with inlay of various woods and ormolu mounts. French, 1775; made by Jean-Henri Riesener for Louis XVI. The marquetry center formerly contained the royal monogram, but the maker altered it after the Revolution. The gilt mounts include caryatid figures of Prudence, Temperance, Mars, and Hercules in a manner approaching full-round sculpture. Musée Condé, Chantilly.

129 *(below)* So-called *Bureau du Roi*, a cylinder writing table with marquetry of various woods and ormolu mounts, candle brackets, and inset clock. French, 1760–63; commissioned by Louis XV from Jean-François Oeben and completed by Jean-Henri Riesener. The mounts were designed by Duplessis; the clock, by Lépine. Palace of Versailles.

130 Pier glass of carved pine and gilded gesso.
English, c. 1735; probably designed by William
Kent and executed by Benjamin Goodison for
Frederick, Prince of Wales, whose emblem it
bears. Victoria and Albert Museum, London.

131 Side table of carved pine and gilded gesso,
bearing baronial arms of Sir Richard Temple.
English, c. 1715; probably by James Moore.
Victoria and Albert Museum, London.

The Protestant North

As was stated in the preface, this book has been designed in sections, each illustrating what may be described as one of the main themes in the development of Western furniture since the Renaissance. This necessarily involves some shuttling back and forth in time, especially in the late 17th and early 18th centuries, when so many styles ran concurrently in Europe.

The opening illustrations of this portion (pp. 82, 87–88) show a brief encounter of the Anglo-Dutch Protestant world with baroque at the time of Louis XIV. Even though there is some ebullience of decoration, it is handled quite differently from the Italian tradition, both in scale and inspiration.

The contrasting simplicity of the Anglo-Dutch style, which took over in the North at the turn of the century, is immediately apparent in the succeeding pages. Even if a little lacquer or a little inlay is allowed to enliven the surface of some pieces, the lines and construction are normally as simple as could be. In the majority of pieces from this time, only the grain, color, and texture of the actual woods relieve their puritan simplicity. Some transatlantic versions, spanning roughly the same period, are then shown (pp. 96–97).

In other Northern Protestant lands, especially the German areas, some taste for baroque decorative elements remained. In these last, it is not surprising that a movement of such vitality as the Southern rococo should make its influence felt, and our illustrations (pp. 98–103) make these penetrations clear. Elements of rococo are also found in certain of the American rooms of the era (pp. 104–107).

The English pieces that follow (pp. 108–119) show the opening of another, and more purely English, style which was to have much influence. The examples given here mainly date from about the second quarter of the 18th century. The work of the previous decades has been modified by Continental influences or classical and Palladian studies. But, in spite of this, there remains a basic austerity far removed from what was then happening in France or Italy, or in any other areas under their influence.

If the pope had been the Protestants' bogey man for the first half of the 17th century, his place was ably taken by King Louis XIV in the latter decades. In fact, the French monarch was anathema to a great many other people as well. He frightened the Holy Roman emperor, swallowed up Spain, raided the Low Countries, bribed the English, and generally meddled in anybody's affairs he decided to make his own. With all this show of power, there naturally came fear and hate along with the deep respect generated in many princely hearts. Lesser rulers everywhere modeled themselves after the magnificent Louis, and for a century or more he became the hero of most princelings. No one before, it seemed, had ever been so splendid. No one had ever held such courts. No one got more out of his subjects and to all appearances had less trouble—at the start anyway.

If all this and the glitter and absolutism of Versailles were naturally appealing to those of royal descent, it presented the antithesis of what the world should be for any puritan or democrat. Someone had to oppose the ogre, and for this role fate chose no handsome, dashing Siegfried but a small, morose, Dutch homosexual who managed to maintain the honor of his house and also to acquire the English crown as well, so frightened were that country's people of a papist convert in the French king's pay who should legitimately have succeeded his brothers.

These mixed attitudes were extremely important to the homemakers of the late 17th and early 18th centuries. As was suggested in the preceding section, the Louis-oriented princes sought to set themselves as near his grandeur as resources would permit and copied the French styles and ways. And where they led, their subjects followed.

In opposition, the Northern countries set their course toward a much austerer dignity—if not quite grandeur—of their own, occasionally following a short flirtation with baroque, as in the silver furniture of William III. But if "Dutch William" had himself new wings at Hampton Court or Kensington, their interiors received quite another treatment from the style of Versailles. Instead of stucco, gold, and damask, there was likely to be sheer oak paneling with nothing but its nice proportions sketched in by a line of moulding, and for greater rooms, perhaps, a band of lightly carved leaf cornice to enhance the atmosphere of dignified restraint. In place of the turned chairs and lacquer and inlays and swags and putti of the Restoration came the plainest sweep of oak or walnut supported on a tasteful scroll for legs or stretchers.

If an artist like Thornhill did a painted ceiling such as that at Greenwich, the simplest of lovely pillars supported it to set it off as a picture in a frame, as something detached and apart and in direct opposition to the flaming baroque hurly-burly that sought to carry its viewers off to Arcadia or Hell.

This Northern tendency to simplicity was to last as a basic feature right through the span of a century. Whatever frivolous decoration or furnishings might be designed for occasional less Tory patrons, such works were always in a minority, partly no doubt for reasons of cost but also very much on grounds of taste.

In England this Dutch style softened, and indeed ennobled, Commonwealth restraint. It ousted what little there was of baroque penetration, except in minor decoration here and there. By the time the century had turned, it had blended into the English classical tradition which showed so beautifully in buildings from Inigo Jones to Christopher Wren. The result in furniture was that charming, gracious, modest half-Dutch taste that the English call Queen Anne. With its gentle forms and pride in wood and craftsmanship, it was for a time to influence the world, and most particularly North America—where it lasted in one form or another almost without interruption, even till today. For balance, taste, and modesty, for what one might call its unostentatious breeding, it is

still the Protestants' delight; and if more robust personalities would prefer brighter styles, those who play safe can never have enough of it. Certainly the simple basic forms—the high-backed chairs with graceful cabriole legs, the plain chests of drawers so quietly functional (if you can stoop), the tallboys or highboys, tables, desks, and all the rest—which came from England or the Netherlands took hold throughout the North. They even penetrated into rococo realms and down to Italy itself, whence some inspiration also came. This was a two-way influence, since it seems most likely that the charming painted Venetian pieces or even certain forms from Naples would not have been quite as they were without this exchange. Above all, in provincial pieces, where baroque fantasy would be costly as well as out of taste, the Northern forms, lightened by rococo motifs in their carved or painted decoration, lasted in peasant work for generations.

While cherishing a basic simplicity, through their inherited classical interests English designers were destined to be led off into another rather special field in the second quarter of the 18th century, into the style usually known as Palladian or Kent. While the first examples of this taste were fairly limited and were confined to some dilettantes and intellectuals, over a longer time the influence was very considerable, especially towards the end of the 19th and the early 20th century, when an English "country house" style often showed more Kentian than other characteristics. Basically an architectural taste, depending in large degree on its architectural features such as pedimented doors and chimneypieces, this was especially suited to the poses of those patrons with a nice conceit of themselves. Later its combination of richness and sobriety made it particularly suitable for those such as banks or large staid companies, for which a background of conservative pomposity was held desirable. Probably more boardrooms of today owe more to William Kent than do the interiors of his own time.

As its name implies, the style was nominally based on the teachings of the Italian Renaissance architect Andrea Palladio; but onto these were grafted "Italianate" incursions by a group for whom Italian travel and Italian art were held to be essential. It favored the ancient orders but, unlike neoclassic attitudes toward the end of the century, tended to use reinterpreted classical ideas and themes rather than to copy them exactly. For example, since earlier busts of emperors and worthies set out in a library unquestionably gave a nice idea of well-bred literacy and distinction, so they *were* set about—though often in a way that might have surprised an old Roman. Motifs of Greek key or wave, if bold enough, were thought to give the same effect. Grafted onto a heavier and bolder use of earlier fielded paneling, they gave proud weight to what might seem a little modest in Queen Anne taste. At its most exaggerated, the style could be a dilettante's agreeable pretense; but little wonder that its basic qualities appealed to persons of more modest station, especially in the provinces and in the colonies. Large, formal, with an air of weight and purpose, the desks, bookcases, tables, and chairs in this style were, as we suggested, just what an increasingly established and self-contented wealthy merchant class felt to be in the right taste. In a way, its roots were not unlike a sort of democratic interpretation of the early Versailles attitudes. Certainly it was in marked distinction to the Régence or Louis XV of contemporary France, or to the then current rococo of Germany. The more traditional furniture which followed through with an elaboration and enrichment of Queen Anne traditions was perhaps nearer to trends on the Continent. The absolute simplicity was varied by addition of Italianate motifs such as masks and shells, as well as borrowings from the same classic grammar of ornament the Kentians had chosen. If there was decorative enrichment, it was probably because the Whig aristocracy, who in effect ruled the country, was becoming very rich. It is interesting that in England the court was to count for very little as an arbiter of taste under alien and, on the whole, unsympathetic monarchs. A small group allied with the Prince of Wales, who was on no terms with his father, set a somewhat more advanced tone in the reign of George II; but in no way did its slightly gayer contributions bear any relation to the best of Continental rococo as introduced at German courts.

The dilettante influences that had evolved Palladian ways were soon to spread in England. Architecture, as we have noted, had always been a study that nobility and gentry and even royalty were fitted to pursue. Now this same approbation was extended to the realm of interior decoration, and as with rococo princes abroad, aristocratic and wealthy patrons were now prepared to take an active part in actual artistic creation. A notable example in England was the group whose studies of history encouraged them to a romantic and idealized taste for Gothic. Horace Walpole is a household name for such associations, but he was far from alone in his interest. The Neogothic start made just before mid-century by these earlier purveyors of the taste was to play an ever-greater part, until it became a dominating feature in the mid-19th century decades.

Chinoiserie and other such exotic rococo tastes soon attracted goodly numbers of designers and their patrons. These tendencies owed much to private dilettante interest. Though dominated rather more by professionals than by dilettantes, the whole movement of neoclassicism that arose in the second half of the 18th century was basically an outgrowth of excavations patronized by rich and scholarly gentlemen and princes. Among those who financed some of the early archaeological expeditions was an English club whose members called themselves frankly the Society of Dilettanti. Together with the various royal academies, which were then stirring everywhere, such groups played an all-important part both in what was occurring and in what was to occur, as we shall perceive in a later section.

132 *(above)* Sleeping chair of carved, painted, and gilded wood, covered in red damask woven with metal thread (adjustable back can be let down for reclining). English, probably mid-17th century (recorded in the house inventory of 1679). Ham House, Surrey.

133 *(right)* Armchair, with carved, painted and gilded frame and Italian silk damask cover. English, c. 1675. Ham House, Surrey.

134 *(above) Chinoiserie* cabinet, japanned in imitation of Chinese lacquerwork and set on carved and silvered wooden stand. English, c. 1670–80. Victoria and Albert Museum, London.

135 *(below)* Carved walnut armchair, with cane seat and back. English, c. 1685. The florid carving shows mixed French and Dutch influences. Victoria and Albert Museum, London.

136 *(right)* Lacquered furniture in Ham House, Surrey, near London. English late 17th–18th century. The chairs, mentioned in an inventory of 1683, imitate Chinese forms and lacquerwork. The bookrest matches the chairs; the table is 18th-century.

137 Wooden hall chair, japanned black with decorative gilt borders. English, first quarter of 18th century (coats of arms probably painted later). Victoria and Albert Museum, London.

139 *(above)* Carved wood dining chair, japanned in Chinese mode with gold on black ground. English, c. 1725. Museo Nazionale di Capodimonte, Naples.

140 Dining chair, japanned in scarlet with gilt *chinoiserie*. English, c. 1710. Victoria and Albert Museum, London.

138 English furniture japanned in Chinese manner on a scarlet ground: secrétaire-cabinet with mirrored doors, early 18th century; clock, signed "Windmill Londoni," c. 1725; caned daybed, made by Giles Grendey, c. 1730. Victoria and Albert Museum, London.

143 *(right)* Walnut dining chair, with back and seat rails veneered and cabriole legs carved of solid wood. English, c. 1730. Victoria and Albert Museum, London.

141 Cabinet veneered with burr maple. English, c. 1690 (legs restored). The floral marquetry panels show Dutch influence. Victoria and Albert Museum, London.

142 Walnut-veneer cabinet with floral marquetry (upper part containing 23 drawers). English, c. 1700. Victoria and Albert Museum, London.

144 Clock of lacquered wood. Danish, second quarter of 18th century; the works are signed by Peter Mathiesen, active in Copenhagen. The cabinetwork is inspired by English and Dutch models of that period. Nationalmuseet, Copenhagen.

145 *(left)* Walnut-veneer secrétaire-cabinet, with panels of arabesque marquetry and a central panel of flowers in etched and stained woods. Perhaps made in England by an immigrant Dutch craftsman, c. 1700(?). Victoria and Albert Museum, London.

147 *(above)* Dressing table on stand (so-called "Union Suite"), of burr-maple veneer bordered with kingwood, in form of a swing mirror atop miniature bureau. English, c. 1720. Victoria and Albert Museum, London.

146 *(above)* Walnut tallboy, with carved corners and cabriole legs. English, c. 1730. The claw-and-ball feet have inlaid ivory nails. Victoria and Albert Museum, London.

148 *(right)* Walnut slant-front bureau, with carved mouldings and claw-and-ball feet. English, c. 1730. Victoria and Albert Museum, London.

149 Wing chair with walnut cabriole legs, covered
with needlework (taken from design published
in 1658). English, c. 1710–20.
Victoria and Albert Museum, London.

150 *(above)* Walnut slant-front bureau-cabinet.
English, c. 1725; signed by the cabinetmaker
Samuel Bennett. The upper part has panels of
arabesque marquetry in a style surviving
from a decade earlier. Victoria and Albert
Museum, London.

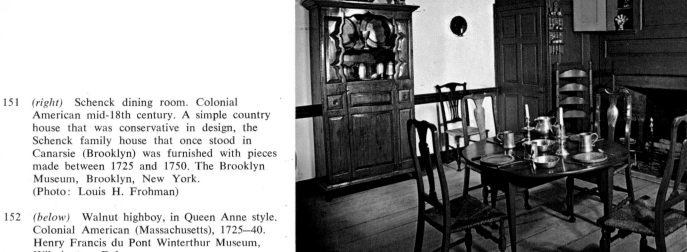

151 *(right)* Schenck dining room. Colonial American mid-18th century. A simple country house that was conservative in design, the Schenck family house that once stood in Canarsie (Brooklyn) was furnished with pieces made between 1725 and 1750. The Brooklyn Museum, Brooklyn, New York. (Photo: Louis H. Frohman)

152 *(below)* Walnut highboy, in Queen Anne style. Colonial American (Massachusetts), 1725–40. Henry Francis du Pont Winterthur Museum, Wilmington, Delaware.

153 Parlor, or common room, from Vauxhall
Gardens, Greenwich (formerly Cohansie),
New Jersey. Colonial American, 1700–25.
The imposing fireplace is framed with a heavy
wood moulding and 17th-century Delft tiles.
The larger pieces are mainly Philadelphia
furniture in Queen Anne style; the walnut
high chest of drawers dates from about 1750.
Henry Francis du Pont Winterthur Museum,
Wilmington, Delaware.

154 Queen Anne japanned highboy. Colonial
American (Boston), c. 1735. Metropolitan
Museum of Art, New York.

155 Walnut slant-front bureau, with raised cabinet flanked by carved sidepieces. Dutch, first half of 18th century. Rijksmuseum, Amsterdam.

156 Walnut wardrobe (*Dielen Schränke*), overlaid with high-relief carving in contrasting wood. North German, c. 1700. Schloss Petronell, Austria (property of Kunsthistorisches Museum, Vienna).

158 Commode with marquetry of natural and stained woods, gilt mounts, and marble top. Danish, 1720–40. Nationalmuseet, Copenhagen.

159 Slant-front bureau, inlaid with fruitwood on figured-walnut ground, with marquetry figures and cartouches. Italian (Lombardy), mid-18th century. Private collection, Milan.

157 Long-case clock of stained elmwood, with ebony mouldings. Dutch, second quarter of 18th century; signed Roger Dunster. The giltwood figures represent Atlas and two Victories. Victoria and Albert Museum, London.

99

160 Mahogany chair, with carved cabriole legs and backrest. Dutch, second quarter of 18th century. Victoria and Albert Museum, London.

161 *(above)* Commode-cabinet, with burr-walnut veneer and rococo carved details. Dutch, mid-18th century. Rijksmuseum, Amsterdam.

162 (left) Commode-cabinet with burr-walnut veneer, inlaid with other rare woods. Dutch, c. 1750. The mounts are silver, and the mirror panels are painted with aquatic birds in imitation of Chinese export work. Rijksmuseum, Amsterdam.

163 (below) Birdcage of blue-and-white delftware. Dutch, late 17th–early 18th century. The importance assumed by delftware pieces in Dutch interiors of this period allows one to consider a fine ceramic such as this in the category of household furnishings. Rijksmuseum, Amsterdam.

164 *(below)* Solid walnut wardrobe, with owners' coat of arms incised inside. German (Frankfurt), first half of 18th century. Wolters Collection, Frankfurt.

165 *(above)* Commode, veneered with burr walnut and set on carved legs. German (Frankfurt), mid-18th century. J. Böhler Gallery, Munich.

166 *(below)* Commode with panels of cube parquetry. German (Franconia), c. 1750–60. J. Böhler Gallery, Munich.

167　Walnut-veneer wardrobe, with pilaster motif.
German (Frankfurt), second quarter of
18th century. Wolters Collection, Frankfurt.

168 Parlor of Philipsburg Manor, Upper Mills
(North Tarrytown), New York. Colonial
American, late 17th–early 18th century.
The room contains a mixture of Dutch and
American furniture of the period; the painted
sideboard is mid-18th century.
(Photo: Louis H. Frohman)

169 So-called "Palladian Drawing Room," Gunston
Hall (home of George Mason), Lorton, Virginia.
Colonial American, 1758; by William Buckland.
This family room, intended for playing games
and informal entertaining, is considered
Buckland's masterpiece, with its elaborate
carving and Palladian broken pediments above
niches and doors.

170 (above) Sitting room (museum reconstruction).
American, first quarter of 19th century.
The sewing chair with side drawers and the
early pine secretary are noteworthy here.
The Shaker Museum, Old Chatham, New York.
(Photo: Louis H. Frohman)

172 *(above)* So-called "Fraktur Room," using
mottled blue woodwork from farmhouse near
Kutztown (Berks County), Pennsylvania.
American (Pennsylvania German), 1783;
built by David Hottenstein. The books and
walls of the room display samples of
Fraktur-schriften, the German medieval art of
illuminated writing that persisted in
Pennsylvania till the mid-19th century.
Henry Francis du Pont Winterthur Museum,
Wilmington, Delaware.

171 *(left)* So-called "Pottery Room" (museum
reconstruction). American, in a style of about
1800. This white-plastered room, created as
a setting for a collection of mainly 19th-century
American pottery, is partly inspired by a
plate in Owen Biddle's *The Young Carpenter's
Assistant* (Philadelphia, 1805). The spare
furnishings stand on an American striped
cotton rug, and the corner double doors are
from a Lancaster (Pennsylvania) church.
Henry Francis du Pont Winterthur Museum,
Wilmington, Delaware.

107

173 *(above)* Mahogany slant-front bureau on stand, with shaped brass handles and keyplates. English, second quarter of 18th century. Victoria and Albert Museum, London.

175 *(right)* Armchair of Brazilian rosewood, with brass inlay. English, c. 1740; attributed to John Channon. Victoria and Albert Museum, London.

174 *(left)* Carved mahogany desk, similar to the style of William Vile. English, mid-18th century. Victoria and Albert Museum, London.

176 *(above)* Mahogany side table, with rosewood and brass inlay. English, c. 1740; attributed to John Channon. Brass-fitted box atop table is probably by the same craftsman. Victoria and Albert Museum, London.

177 Mahogany bureau-cabinet, with brass inlay; other materials used include rosewood and tortoise shell. English, c. 1740; attributed to John Channon. Victoria and Albert Museum, London.

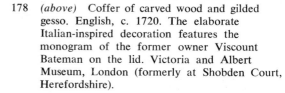

178 *(above)* Coffer of carved wood and gilded gesso. English, c. 1720. The elaborate Italian-inspired decoration features the monogram of the former owner Viscount Bateman on the lid. Victoria and Albert Museum, London (formerly at Shobden Court, Herefordshire).

179 Dining chair of carved softwood and gilded gesso, covered with Italian cut velvet of the period. English, after 1715 (bears coat of arms of William Humphreys, Lord Mayor of London in 1717). Victoria and Albert Museum, London.

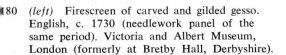

180 (left) Firescreen of carved and gilded gesso.
English, c. 1730 (needlework panel of the
same period). Victoria and Albert Museum,
London (formerly at Bretby Hall, Derbyshire).

181 (above) Cabinet with panels of Japanese
lacquer and gilded brass hinges. English, c. 1715.
The gilded wood base was probably made by
James Moore. Victoria and Albert Museum,
London (formerly in Kensington Palace).

182 Carved and gilded torchère. English, c. 1730.
This type of piece was originally intended as a
candelabrum stand. Victoria and Albert
Museum, London.

183 *(left)* Ornamental mirror, carved and gilded. English, c. 1730. The piece included a bracket for a clock, a barometer, and a thermometer. The clock (c. 1720), japanned black and gold, is signed "Marwick, London." Victoria and Albert Museum, London.

184 *(below)* Coffer, japanned black and gold in Chinese style and supported by elaborately carved dragons. English, c. 1740. Victoria and Albert Museum, London.

185 *(above)* Detail of intarsia side table. English-Italian, second quarter of 18th century. The intricate marble inlay *(scagliola)*, made in Leghorn about 1726 for the Earl of Litchfield, incorporates his coat of arms and that of his wife. The base of carved and gilded wood was probably ordered about the same time, in England, to support the Italian marble top. Victoria and Albert Museum, London.

186 *(right)* Console table of carved and gilded wood with marble top. English, c. 1740; in the style of William Kent. The elaborately carved eagle base would seem a harbinger of later neoclassic developments on the Continent. Victoria and Albert Museum, London.

187 *(left)* Carved wooden settee, painted and partly gilded. English, c. 1735; probably designed by William Kent. The faun mask carved at the ends of the arms seems to have been a favorite motif of Kent.

188 *(below)* Marble-topped side table of white painted wood, boldly carved with acanthus leaves, foxes, and a female mask. English, c. 1730; probably designed by William Kent. Victoria and Albert Museum, London (from Coleshill House, Berkshire).

189 Wall cabinet, veneered in
tulipwood and inset with ivories.
English, 1743. This piece was
made for Horace Walpole's
collection of miniatures. The
statuettes of Rubens, Duqesnoy,
and Van Dyck are modeled after
Rysbrack; the ivory reliefs are of
the 17th and 18th centuries.
Victoria and Albert Museum,
London.

190 *(below)* Carved walnut chair with cabriole legs, partly gilded. English, c. 1730. Victoria and Albert Museum, London.

191 *(right)* Carved and gilded dining chair, with dolphins on legs and backrest. English, c. 1730. Victoria and Albert Museum, London.

192 *(right)* Solid mahogany dining chair, carved with lion heads and feet. English, c. 1725–30 (needlework cover of backrest and seat is of the same period). Leicester Museums and Art Gallery.

193 *(left)* Carved mahogany armchair, with veneered back. English, c. 1730. The leonine motif also dominates this finely carved chair. Victoria and Albert Museum, London.

194 *(below)* Carved mahogany settee; partly gilded. English, c. 1740; attributed to William Kent. Victoria and Albert Museum, London (formerly at Wroxton Abbey, Oxfordshire).

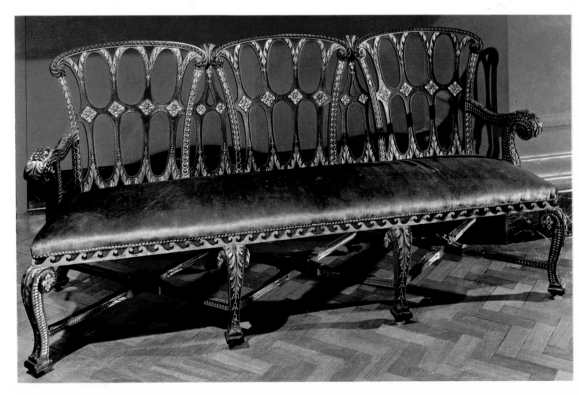

195 Room from house in Great George Street,
Westminster (London), with pine paneling
painted cream. English, second quarter of 18th
century. Of the same period, the furniture
includes a "spider" table, a carved and painted
bookshelf, and a mahogany bench with
claw-and-ball feet. The embroidered wing
chair and upholstered firescreen are also of the
period. The needlework carpet is English.
Victoria and Albert Museum, London.

197 *(left)* Carved and gilded throne chair, covered with scarlet velvet. Italian (Venetian), c. 1730; almost certainly made from design of Antonio Corradini. Ca' Rezzonico, Venice.

198 *(above)* Miniature armchair of gilded wood. Italian (Venetian), late 17th century. This opulent, boldly carved chair undoubtedly shows some Dutch influence. Villa Rezzonico, near Venice.

Rococo

(Plates 197—262)

The two previous sections have shown how the late 17th and early 18th centuries witnessed one development in France and quite another in the North. This section follows the sequence of events chiefly in the Catholic-dominated areas of northern Italy, South Germany, and Austria. In the Bavarian-Austrian sphere, the rococo movement reached a particularly happy solution. The introductory section, which gave the background of our study, illustrated the first baroque influences coming from Italy to other lands; in Italian areas, as in Spain and Portugal, baroque style lasted virtually through the 18th century. The opening plates here (pp. 120, 125–129) afford some illustration of the innovations of rococo in more northerly regions, where for conservative tastes the style often flourished right up to the end of the 18th century or beyond.

What developed from all this can readily be seen in the next series of plates (pp. 130–139). Italian baroque lay at the root of this development, but a debt was also acknowledged and paid to French inspiration and design books. Nonetheless, there is no doubt that between the Piedmont and Franconia and beyond a different spirit, a greater lustfulness—and even heaviness—arose than would have found favor in courtly France. In a sequence of picture spreads, the distinctive range of both areas is evident (pp. 136–139), as against some later German examples from the third quarter of the century (pp. 140–141).

In so far as anything rococo was allowed to enter the more solemn English scene, German or something other than French inspiration was generally preferred (pp. 142–143). The fundamental difference in the contemporary French developments, shown in the succeeding plates (pp. 144–148), is most strikingly marked in the juxtaposition of two nearly contemporary French and Italian aristocratic interiors (pp. 148–149). A selection of Italian and Iberian pieces of the period concludes this section (pp. 150–155).

Though used in the 18th century and said to stem from *rocaille*—the fake dripping rocks on fountains—the word "rococo" has only rather recently come back into general English use. Even then, it is often made to cover a multitude of creations, mainly dating from the second or third quarters of the 18th century, which sometimes seem to have little in common beyond the name we have given the lot.

Admittedly, the looser use of the word "baroque," which served so long to designate everything created from about 1550 to 1750, was an even broader categorizing. This casualness may well have stemmed from long dislike of the productions of the one or the other for half a century or more, but this does not excuse being slovenly in our usage today. The issue of rococo is also confused in that, although the movement was largely confined to the European mainland (and to Catholic lands at that), it showed marked variation even in its day. For example, an enchanting little putto holding up a reading desk on plate may have some relationship with French ormolu or even sculpture of the time, but it is quite different from any piece of contemporary French furniture. By the same token, none but the wildest productions of the Paris *ébénistes* of Louis XV really appears to speak the same language as the fantasies of Munich or Dresden or of dozens of churches from Weyarn to Vienna. Yet people call them all rococo.

On the fairly rare occasions when Chippendale departed from his austerer English ways to do something in the "French" or "Chinese" taste, it is striking, apart from direct pastiches of Paris, how unlike work from France these native pieces are. Drawn out by somebody like Locke or Darly, they show far more affinity with Germany than Paris. For the *Director* Chippendale did, of course, lift designs from both French and German books.

All in all, if the word "rococo" has come back into our vocabulary, it would seem to have come back rather loosely defined, so that some review is justified, not so much on account of the word but for appreciation of its reflections as shown in the furniture. If, as it does to many people, rococo means all the varieties of Louis XV, then we should perhaps seek some other word for the enchanting developments from baroque that appear in southern German areas. Alternatively, what might seem more reasonable is to call these last "rococo," as being more exaggerated, like the fountain rocks, and to regard the French as a development out of Versailles. This is what we have done here, for if Paris was the center of fashionable taste for the Continent, the influence of the Versailles tradition was very powerful.

The formal court ways were still maintained for more ceremonious occasions; and despite a period of return to Paris under the Regency, which had some effect in modifying the heritage of Louis XIV, his spirit was everywhere at Versailles, and Louis XV went back to pick up the thread. At the same time, in private, he or his mistress led in the reaction toward a change to easier, wittier modes, conforming with the newer attitudes to life conveyed for the period by the word *intime*. Although the word had far wider connotations than "intimacy" in the ordinary English sense, it is not inapposite to suggest that it would be difficult to imagine oneself being "intimate" in the Salle des Glaces to the degree of practicing the arts of gallantry, or even sniggering over the secret erotic picture in a snuffbox or just talking smut—all among the favorite 18th-century delights. These would somehow be inhibited by the reserve of Lebrun, but not by the art of a Fragonard. If this is an exaggerated example, it can nonetheless help in some appreciation of the period. The whole helps one to comprehend how the old Boulle models could still flourish alongside those of Goudreau or Dubois, as also to grasp why most *ébénistes* purveyed their work in many tastes.

Yet, in almost all, the tenor was poised and even formal, which is why we have kept the French examples apart in setting out the plates for this section. In making this distinction, it should be emphasized that our subject is furniture. Were it metalwork or textiles or some other craft such a distinction might be harder to maintain. Indeed, even in the details of marquetry or mounts, there is a much closer similarity among the lot, perhaps because of common engraved sources for so many of the designs and the presence of German craftsmen everywhere.

What, then, was the rococo picture outside France? Naturally enough, the Protestant Northerners in general disapproved of most of it. As we see, a traditional conservative simplicity remained predominant in their areas. Only for a rarer clientele did anything approaching rococo find acceptance there, unless in such decorative adjuncts as mirrors, frames, or candelabra or the twist of ornament slipped in here and there as cresting on a chair or desk.

The mainstream of what we have termed rococo centers on the Catholic German lands and parts of northern Italy, especially in Piedmont (then part of the Kingdom of Sardinia) and Venice. There would seem to be opportunity for study on the relationships between these areas. Despite some acknowledged debt to France, the craftsmen working for the House of Savoy adhered quite clearly to South German ways, and these in turn owed much to North Italian painters and architects. Again, furniture and furnishings from Turin, Munich, Dresden, Vienna, or even Berlin would appear related to each other but, apart from a general period affinity, often are not very like the mainstream deriving from Paris.

But to return to the German rococo development. An old professor once suggested that the best rococo is to be found in wine-drinking countries. How far this contention can be taken seriously might be open to question. Can Bavaria, for instance, be regarded as wine-drinking country? Nevertheless, the idea is a pleasant one to toy with. It somehow suits the style, as far as it can be defined at all, and can at least serve to emphasize that it was a taste never passionately adopted by the North. Certainly, to pick up a thread from our own introduction, rococo is not a Protestant manifestation. Above all, one might say that rococo is atmosphere much more than just a set of rules for design.

The special evolution in German areas was perfectly logical. Though many had emerged from virtual barbarism in one generation, any duke or prince who could, essayed to take on something of the Versailles magnificence and gather about him his richer subjects to make a court, as background to himself instead of being a worrisome burden along the confines of his territory. But these people were not French. French formality and its polite restraints, as opposed to sheer discipline, were foreign traits to them. For the most part, they desired a freer and gayer way—and got it. By the second decade of the 18th century most rulers of any significance had managed to bring even some of their cruder subjects into a fairy world of unreality where conversation took the place of arms. Parties, musical entertainments such as operas and masques, balls, banquets, and picnics took up the time that might otherwise have been spent in plotting difficulties for the ruler, if not outright insurrection. If the whole purpose as in France was to turn the upper classes into playboy puppets, it was succeeding, so that we should not be surprised at finding that these folk liked to make themselves a theater world of fairytale make-believe whose walls might be of painted silk or mirror glass, with golden floral swags and china dolls and ormolu and unreality. The more architectural forms of courtly furnishing were abandoned in favor of a sugarcake delight. The world of lambrequins and volutes, of order and dignity, gave place to a world of wit in which fanciful Chinese, dancers, actors, or monkeys could all play with garlands, spin ribbons, and twist foliage to suit a thousand pretty conceits. Even in the Church itself, the saints and angels joined the fun. The awesome populations of a baroque "other world" became a riotous throng in the clouds where 18th-century religion sought for joy and elegance, and even for gaiety, rather than the Hell and devils of what had gone before.

Even in the international, intellectual aspects of the Age of Enlightenment, the rococo spirit might deliberately turn quite a number of things topsy-turvy. The greatest monarch-general of his day saw nothing "sissy" about doing up a garlanded bedroom like a pretty woman's garden cottage to entertain the leading atheist republican: for that is what really occurred with Frederick the Great and Voltaire. The French king's lovely mistress gave her backing to a style that every prince and duchess thereafter adopted. Diderot, once editor of the greatest scientific publication the world had ever seen, could criticize in print an artist friend's exhibition at the Royal Academy by comparing it, in fullest and quite unexpurgated detail, with the vaunted sexual prowess of a mutual friend. Nobody was shocked, and everyone delighted indeed at the witty thought. And that too was rococo. An Orthodox empress might deck out her stalwart soldier lovers in a galaxy of diamond orders. And all this was often done—most sincerely—in the name of Jesus Christ.

From the standpoint of furniture design, it was essentially the sculptor's rather than the painter's day

for form, though not always for decoration. While designs might still depend upon the pen-and-wash sketch as with the baroque, their execution was for modelers and carvers, not only for the actual scrollwork and figures, gilded metal mounts, or broken pediments but in their spirit as well. Rococo furniture does not really stand discreetly up against a wall, as might the picture hung above it. Such extravagant pieces seem to stride into the room or, in many cases, were made to stand straight up in the middle of it.

Where the painter did enter into it was in the use of color, as our selection of plates clearly shows. Whether on the walls or in the silks, embroidery, or jewels, colors—usually what may perhaps be called just "lovely" colors, rather than "forceful" or "strident" as before—rioted everywhere in rococo interiors, whether it be in the ceilings of Tiepolo or in the furniture of Venice or of Cuvilliés. To accentuate the color, moreover, generous amounts of gold and silver were introduced. Natural woods, except for the very finest used as veneers or inlays, marquetry and parquetry, were normally eschewed other than in lesser or provincial work. Paint, lacquer, *vernis martin*, and so on—these covered every object the princes of the rococo era were to have around them. When paint appeared on the paneling of one court, we are told that eleven, or maybe twelve, of the thinnest separate coats were usually applied. One commentator declared it was in order that the nostrils of princesses should not be offended. Perhaps so, but since paint thinner stinks as much as anything—except perhaps the persons, rooms, and passages of many undrained 18th-century palaces—this rationale seems a little odd.

The enormous cost of a splendid rococo palace or pavilion, or even a theater, of any size at all was so prodigious that it meant, as with baroque, that the style was only a very rich man's hobby, something strictly for millionaires or princes of higher rank, whether laymen or churchmen. What trickled down to ordinary folk, even of the upper classes, might be a plaster ceiling with motifs of some gaiety, or furnishings that were above-average in fancy decoration. Further down, the influence was mainly in the way of fabrics or decorative motifs, such as scrolls and crestings, and in the use of tasteful curves in chairs, tables, chests, cupboards, clocks, and such. A freer use of color also reached the peasantry, and the charming rural houses with their painted shutters and doors would not continue to please us today had it not been for artists such as Cuvilliés, Oppenord, or

123

Tiepolo, or such gay and sprightly patrons as Madame de Pompadour.

That rococo creations were so exaggerated and expensive certainly makes clear that, whoever made the designs, the princes' and patrons' personal participation must have been both detailed and considerable. To order a rococo church or chapel or ballroom or theater was scarcely like going to a nice, safe "reputable" firm of architects with the assurance that you would get something like the Joneses or the Browns had, something discreetly within your purse limits and status aspirations. In broaching the point of royal participation in an earlier passage, we gave as notable examples Frederick the Great, the Elector Max Emanuel, and Lothar Franz von Schönborn. From their documents we know how intimately concerned they felt in such aesthetic choices. They were all patrons of the best rococo artists they could get, but there must have been a host of other clients, from abbots of great monasteries on down to parish clergy. Some of the latter, so that their village church might be rebuilt, even drafted parishioners in "voluntary" work on such projects. Then, if they could not get one of the celebrated Asams, they found a village carver or painter to decorate the walls and ceilings and make the statues. Charming and nostalgic though some of their handiwork remains for us today, it also underlines the fact that, to achieve the best in this most elaborate of styles, only the finest craftsmen would really do. This applies as much to individual objects as to an entire church.

If this seems something of a digression from the more restricted field of furniture, it serves to point up one great essential of the style. Above all with rococo, every part or element was a vital contribution to the whole, from walls and floors and ceilings to chairs, tables, and commodes, or even the locks and gratings. Such special furniture, then, cannot look the same outside its original setting; at the time it would quite probably have been designed by its purveyor or even an architect who arranged the decoration of the entire room down to the smallest detail. It was said in Paris that if you bought a house you had to buy the furniture as well, since nothing else would fit. This shows even more vividly in the reverse case: where a marvelous room may have been restored but lacks its original furnishings, or has merely some inferior replacements, and the end result looks both lost and sad, no matter how imposing the space.

Even where the setting and objects are intact, rococo needs its suitable occupants in appropriate clothes and jewelry, moving about in their colored silks, with ceremonious or brittle and witty mien. Perhaps it is because of its demands, as well as its cost, that even in its time the finest of genuinely rococo furniture was very limited in quantity. Not many persons could meet these demands. More conventional interiors arranged with simpler objects make less demand upon one's purse or personality. Certainly, at its most extreme, full rococo was fundamentally for occasional special use and not intended as something "to live in every day" or to use continuously. A church or a theater—forms closely allied to the rococo mind—or a state room or love pavilion were all perfect subjects for the style. No one, unless immensely poised *and* philistine, could really take off his hunting boots and then stand warming himself before the fireplace in a rococo salon! What could be inhibiting in the most elaborate variants also extends in some way to the lesser adaptations made for more ordinary people.

199 Carved walnut side table, partly
gilded. Italian (Lombardy), third
quarter of 17th century;
attributed to Andrea Fantoni.
In such highly sculptural baroque
furniture as this and the table
below, the functional purpose is
obscured by the virtuoso carving.
Accademia Carrara, Bergamo.

200 Console table of carved and
gilded wood. Italian (Piedmont),
late 17th century. Palazzo Reale,
Turin.

201 *(above)* Armchair carved in boxwood and ebony, covered with needlework. Italian (Venetian), early 18th century; made by Andrea Brustolon for the Venier di San Vio family. Ca' Rezzonico, Venice.

202 *(right)* Armchair of carved and gilded wood. Italian (Venetian), c. 1730; by the sculptor Antonio Corradini. Ca' Rezzonico, Venice.

203 *(above)* Side table of carved and
gilded wood. Italian (Venetian),
early 18th century; probably by
Antonio Corradini. Cini Collection,
Venice.

204 *(right)* Side table of carved and gilded wood.
Italian (Venetian), early 18th century; the
clock, of later date, is signed "Aless. Bertolla,
Venezia." Ca' Rezzonico, Venice.

205 (above) Carved and painted wooden bed. German, c. 1700. Bayerisches Nationalmuseum, Munich.

206 (below) Painted wooden bench. Italian, early 18th century. This piece has characteristics of provincial South German design and decoration, with great emphasis on the coats of arms flanking a heraldic eagle. Palazzo d'Arco, Mantua.

207 Bedroom of Prince Eugene of Savoy
(1663–1736). Austrian, second quarter of
18th century. The lavish decor of this
bedchamber includes large-scale murals and
painted panels and stuccoes on the ceiling.
The carved, gilded and painted bed and the
typical huge Austrian stove have figures
alluding to the military victories of this famous
general. Monastery of St. Florian, Austria.

208 *(left)* Writing table veneered with tortoise shell, silver, and brass. German, c. 1700; made for Max Emanuel, Elector of Bavaria. Bayerisches Nationalmuseum, Munich.

209 Bureau desk encased in gilt brass, brilliantly inlaid with classical scenes in lapis lazuli, *pietre dure*, and mother-of-pearl. French, c. 1710; perhaps made by Domenico Cucci, an Italian working at the Gobelins. López-Willshaw Collection, Paris.

210 "Red Damask Room" at Schloss
Charlottenburg, Berlin. German, early 18th
century; built for the Electress Sophia Charlotte. 131
The walls are hung with rich red fabric, with
appliqué panel designs of gold braid.
Architectural detail is restrained baroque.

211 Carved and gilded console table, with veined marble top. German (Bavaria), c. 1730; design shows influence of François Cuvilliés. Gilt-bronze and alabaster candelabrum is French. Residenzmuseum, Munich.

212 Harpsichord, with case, legs, and stretchers japanned with Chinese scenes on cream ground. German, c. 1710; made in Berlin and intended for court use. Schloss Charlottenburg Berlin.

213 Armchair, painted, gilded, and upholstered in silk damask. German (Bavaria), c. 1730. Residenzmuseum, Munich.

214 Clock decorated with Chinese motifs and scenes on scarlet, blue, and cream grounds (with matching stand). German (Augsburg), c. 1725; clock bears signature of Benedikt Firstenfelder. Bayerisches Nationalmuseum, Munich.

215 Mirrored room in the Residenz, Munich.
German, 1731; designed by François Cuvilliés,
with stuccoes carried out by Johann
B. Zimmerman (restored since 1944). The
furniture, dating mostly from about 1730,
includes a rare console writing table, by
Wilhelm de Groff.

216 *(below)* Lectern of carved, painted, and gilded wood. South German, mid-18th century. Bayerisches Nationalmuseum, Munich.

217 *(above)* Display cabinet of carved, painted, and gilded wood. German (Bavaria), mid-18th century; probably crafted in Munich by J. M. Schmidt, according to designs by Cuvilliés. Residenzmuseum, Munich.

218 Carved and gilded wooden commode. German (Bavaria), 1761. Designed by François Cuvilliés for the Residenz, this piece shows how French rococo underwent a subtle change for German patrons. Residenzmuseum, Munich.

219 *(above)* Writing table, inlaid with various woods and etched ivory. Italian (Piedmont), dated 1741. Museo Correr, Venice.

220 *(left)* Mirrored cabinet set on side table; materials used include walnut, box, ebony, ivory, steel, and mother-of-pearl inlays, with gilt-bronze mounts. Italian (Piedmont), 1731–33. Palazzo Reale, Turin.

221 *(right)* Pedestal for sculpture, inlaid with various woods and ivory. Italian (Piedmont), c. 1740. Palazzo del Quirinale, Rome.

222 *(far right)* Cabinet on console base, inlaid with various woods and ivory. Italian (Piedmont), c. 1740. Palazzina di Caccia, Stupinigi.

223 Walnut-veneer bureau-cabinet, inlaid with ivory and rare woods. South German, 1738. Victoria and Albert Museum, London.

224 Long-case clock of limewood. German (Hamburg), mid-18th century. Carved in an extreme rococo manner, this clock has works signed by the watchmaker Johann Emmrich. Museum für Kunst und Gewerbe, Hamburg.

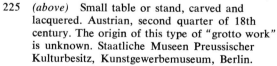

225 *(above)* Small table or stand, carved and lacquered. Austrian, second quarter of 18th century. The origin of this type of "grotto work" is unknown. Staatliche Museen Preussischer Kulturbesitz, Kunstgewerbemuseum, Berlin.

226 *(above right)* Armchair, carved with scrolls and flowers and painted. German, mid-18th century; in the style of J. A. Nahl. Museum für Kunsthandwerk, Frankfurt.

227 *(right)* Walnut cabinet, inlaid with ivory and with legs and cresting of gilded wood. German (Würzburg), 1744; cabinet by Carl M. Mattern, and carved base attributed to G. A. Guthmann. The coat of arms is that of Prince-Bishop Anselm Franz of Ingelheim. Mainfränkisches Museum, Würzburg (copyright by Verlag Gundermann, Würzburg).

139

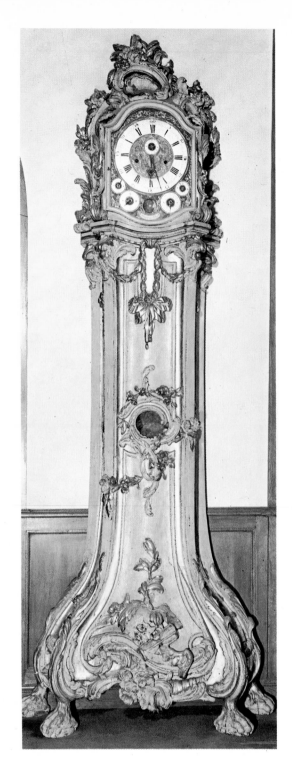

228 Carved long-case clock, painted and gilded. Russian, mid-18th century. The clockworks are signed "Jacob Guldan, Presburg." Galleria Vangelisti, Lucca.

229 Long-case clock, with tulipwood veneer and rococo carving in cherry. German (Berlin), 1770; probably from a design by J. M. Hoppenhaupt. Mounts are of silver-gilt carved wood. Schloss Charlottenburg, Berlin.

230 Painted and gilded armchair, with
     original *petit-point* covering. Polish, mid-18th
     century. Private collection (formerly in
     Radziwill Collection, Warsaw).

231 Commode, with rosewood veneer and
     gilt-bronze mounts. German (Berlin), mid-18th
     century. The triple curve of the cornerpieces
     and legs is especially striking. Schloss
     Charlottenburg, Berlin.

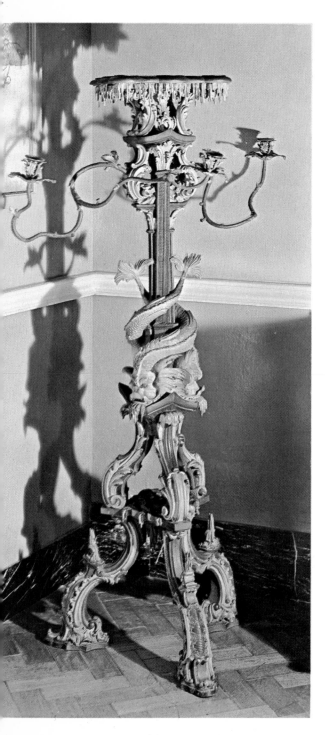

233 Carved pine armchair, painted and gilded. English, second half of 18th century. Francis Stonor Collection, London.

232 *(above)* Torchére of carved and painted softwood. English, c. 1760; follows closely a design by Thomas Johnson published in 1758. Victoria and Albert Museum, London (formerly at Hagley Park, Worcestershire).

234 *(right)* Mahogany writing and dressing table, with rococo mounts of gilded bronze. English, second quarter of 18th century. This was originally one of a pair which, standing back to back, formed a library table. Victoria and Albert Museum, London.

235 (below) Carved wooden console table and pier glass, painted and gilded. English, c. 1745; mirror designed by Matthias Lock. Victoria and Albert Museum, London (formerly in the Tapestry Room of Hinton House, Somerset).

236 (above) Polychrome mirror in Chinese taste, of carved, painted, and gilded pine. English, mid-18th century (possibly by a craftsman-designer from the Continent). Victoria and Albert Museum, London.

237 Commode in *vernis Martin*: originally white and red, now yellowed with the darkened varnish. French, c. 1765; made by Gilles Joubert for Madame Adelaide, daughter of Louis XV. Sold at Sotheby, London, in 1965. (Photo: R. Guillemot, *Connaissance des Arts*)

238 *(left)* Lady's bureau, japanned in Chinese style. French, mid-18th century; from Château de Bellevue, the property of Madame de Pompadour and Louis XV. Musée des Arts Décoratifs, Paris.

239 *(left)* Lady's writing bureau, japanned scarlet and with Chinese scenes in raised gilt; ormolu mounts. German (Mannheim), c. 1770; once belonged to Electress Elisabetta Augusta. Residenzmuseum, Munich.

240 Bed *(lit à la polonaise)* of carved and gilded wood, with original damask coverings. French, mid-18th century; by Nicolas Heurtaut. Palace of Versailles (formerly in Castle of La Tour, Normandy).

241 "Conversation chair" (*voyeuse*). French, mid-18th century (Louis XV period); by Jean Baptiste Tilliard. This type of chair, with a padded "shelf" arrangement atop the backrest, was intended for watching card or other table games, in comfort yet without disturbing the players. Musée des Arts Décoratifs, Paris.

243 *(below)* Chair of painted and gilded wood, upholstered in needlework. French, c. 1755 (Louis XV period); by Jean Baptiste Tilliard. Louvre, Paris (cliché des Musées Nationaux).

242 Dressing chair (*fauteuil à coiffer*) of carved polished wood, with cane seat and backrest. French, mid-18th century (Louis XV period); by Jean Baptiste Boulard. The indented contour of the back and the caning were suited to the purpose of this chair, namely, as a seat used while powdering one's hairdo. Private collection.

245 *(below)* Sofa (*veilleuse*), with carved and painted wooden frame and its original silk brocade covering. French, mid-18th century (Louis XV period); by Jean Nadal. Rijksmuseum, Amsterdam.

244 *(above)* Small loveseat (*marquise*), with moulded frame of gilded wood. French, mid-18th century (Louis XV period); by Louis Delanois. Louvre, Paris.

246 *(below)* *Duchesse brisée*, with gilded wooden frame. French, c. 1765 (Louis XV period); by Louis Delanois. These ensembles consisted of an armchair and one or two other pieces contoured to extend into a *chaise longue*. Louvre, Paris (cliché des Musées Nationaux).

248 "Chinese Room," Palazzo Reale, Turin.
Italian, 1732–36; decorated by Filippo Juvarra.
This interior approaches the ultimate
sophistication and exoticism of the rococo. The
wall panels of Oriental lacquer are set off by
painted and gilded borders. A geometric parquet
floor and illusionistic ceiling paintings complete
the elaborate decor.

247 (left) French room of the rococo period, with
painted wall panels of La Fontaine's fables by
J. B. Oudry (1686–1755). Furniture, French,
mid-18th century: cane armchair (early
Louis XV); marble-topped gilt console (late
Louis XV). Musée des Arts Décoratifs, Paris.

249 Kingwood casket with decorative gilded metal
hinges, lock, and appliqué, set on carved and
gilded wooden stand. Italian (Piedmont),
mid-18th century. Palazzina di Caccia,
Stupinigi.

251 Candle bracket of carved, painted, and
gilded wood. Italian (Piedmont),
c. 1720; possibly designed by Filippo
Juvarra. The deer motif was very likely
inspired by the setting, a richly finished
hunting lodge. Palazzina di Caccia,
Stupinigi.

250 (left) Settee of carved and gilded wood.
Italian (Piedmont), third quarter of 18th
century. Particularly noteworthy is the
fan-shaped back terminating in wide
outward-sloping armrests. Museo Civico, T

252 (left) Marble-topped console table, carved with flowers and figures in rococo style and painted on a white ground. Italian (Genoa), mid-18th century; bears coat of arms of Staglieno family. Galleria Orselli, Florence.

253 (below) Veronese Room, Palazzo Reale, Turin. Italian, mid-18th century. The gold-gilt and stucco wall and ceiling panels and the furniture are all in full rococo manner, sumptuous Italian adaptations of Louis XV style.

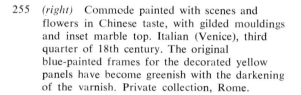

254 *(left)* Side chairs of carved, painted, and gilded wood. Italian (Venice), mid-18th century. Cini Collection, Venice.

255 *(right)* Commode painted with scenes and flowers in Chinese taste, with gilded mouldings and inset marble top. Italian (Venice), third quarter of 18th century. The original blue-painted frames for the decorated yellow panels have become greenish with the darkening of the varnish. Private collection, Rome.

256 *(below)* Daybed with carved wooden frame, painted blue and gilded. Italian (Venice), mid-18th century. Cini Collection, Venice.

257 (above) Conversation group of settee and
two armchairs, with frames japanned yellow
and painted with red flowers echoing the
upholstery fabric. Italian (Venice), mid-18th
century. Ca' Rezzonico, Venice.

258 (below) Commode and armchair, japanned
green and decorated with *chinoiserie* in gilt
gesso. Italian (Venice), mid-18th century.
These are part of a suite of thirty pieces from
Palazzo Calbo-Crotta agli Scalzi. The
hand-painted silk upholstery is of outstanding
quality and subtlety. Ca' Rezzonico, Venice.

259 *(below)* Dining chair, painted with *chinoiserie* on cream ground. Spanish, first half of 18th century. Palace of Aranjuez, near Madrid (by courtesy of Patrimonio Nacional, Madrid).

260 *(above)* Armchair, veneered and inlaid in varied woods. Spanish, third quarter of 18th century; perhaps designed by Matteo Gasparini and executed by the cabinetmaker Canops. Palacio Real, Madrid (by courtesy of Patrimonio Nacional, Madrid).

261 Mahogany chair with tooled leather seat. Portuguese, c. 1750. English and Dutch (here Dutch) influence was strongly evident in much 18th-century Portuguese furniture. Musée des Arts Décoratifs, Paris.

262 Gasparini Salon, Palacio Real, Madrid.
Spanish, late 18th century. The furniture was
made in 1770–80 by Canops, following
designs by Matteo Gasparini (by courtesy
of Patrimonio Nacional, Madrid).

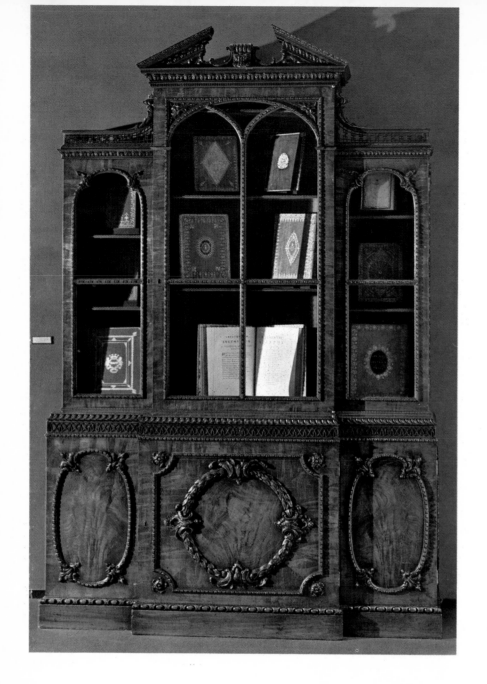

263 (left) Mahogany bookcase, with figured veneer and carved appliqué. English, c. 1760; by William Vile. Victoria and Albert Museum, London (lent by Mrs. Scudamore).

264 Carved mahogany commode. English, c. 1740–50; attributed to William Vile. Victoria and Albert Museum, London.

Great Cabinetmakers

(Plates 263—323)

The exchange of ideas and influences and styles stressed in the notes to the last section became increasingly complicated for the furniture of the second half of the 18th century, and remained so until the more embracing effects of the French Revolution were felt. It is as if there were more concurrent styles, more splinter styles, and more exchange of ideas than there had ever been earlier.

This phenomenon has made the arrangement of the plates fairly arbitrary. But if the illustrations in this section and the next are seen as a broad review of what was happening at the time, if we take into account that all these manifestations were related to one generation, the picture then becomes more reasonable. The first examples (Plates 263–269) show the simple mid-century mahogany pieces from England, which were in themselves something of a novelty. But these also coincide in time with the exoticism of the furnituremaking that follows in sequence (pp. 163–169). Moreover, all these styles are pictured in Chippendale's own catalogue, and his firm would have readily executed any one of them on commission.

If this could happen in one city—and within a single firm—the great differences and variety among the exquisite French workmanship of this era are not surprising (pp. 180–183, 186–189). These examples have been placed here because there would seem to be some evident difference in them, both between the rococo inheritance and the formal court styles. The originality and variety of design, at least in their first instances, may justifiably be held to originate with individual cabinetmakers rather than from any outside dictates of fashion. In this connection it may be significant that many "French" cabinetmakers of this time were foreigners working in Paris.

The illustrations of some more sober American examples (pp. 170–173) represent the solid traditions which continued for the majority, as did the German and Bohemian adherence to native woods and marquetry (pp. 174–178, 190). Even England was affected by Continental taste (pp. 184–185), for there as in Paris foreign craftsmen were also active.

In this section we shall touch on those styles which evolved—part new, part compromise— in the middle decades of the 18th century. The focus here is on England and France, for German and Italian areas in this period tended to carry on in the older baroque-rococo tradition, until the neoclassic takeover at the very end of the century. It is no denigration of what had gone before to suggest that overall, and over all Europe, the middle and later decades of the 18th century saw the apogee of great furnituremaking. This concerned not only the techniques and the craftsmanship, which in the best specimens of the time were unrivaled, but also the taste and, above all, the quality of invention. This was the particular genius of the 18th century.

Centered on London and Paris, the movement was destined to become increasingly international, and it is noteworthy that quite a number of the leading furnituremakers in both London and especially Paris were of foreign origin. As with artists, the situation was rapidly developing away from the old local guild tradition of craftsmanship, and no one cared particularly about nationality provided that the work was good enough.

The overall political background against which these people worked had changed little from the previous decades. Socially, the focus was on a metropolitan society usually centering around a royal or aristocratic court, and from these centers life and fashion spread—and spread with mounting speed. More and more homes, which had hitherto stayed little more than a shelter in which to live, became more a background against which their owners could show themselves to advantage. From the state apartments of princely palaces down to the almost sacrosanct parlors of the bourgeoisie, the purpose was to contrive a fit display of elegance and beauty. Entrance hallways and corridors, rooms, and whole suites were set aside and furnished to make an impression on any who might come to be impressed. This duty done, they were put back under the protection of linen covers. Very pertinent was the comment of an English duke at the opening of this period who, having visited a vast new inheritance, expressed his satisfaction at the state rooms but then was glad to find a much more modest suite which, as he said, would do nicely "for to live in every day."

In all this movement the influence of the courts—and at times of the princes themselves—was extremely important, especially in the promotion of new styles. At the same time, whatever might be the advantages of the blessing of the ruler or an appointment as purveyor to the Crown, unless the royal patronage was active on the scale of an earlier Munich or Dresden, wider support was needed to maintain a thriving industry and lively creative urge in design. This came more and more from a new development of fashion consciousness among leaders of society. Their motives, which may have been as mixed as in any metropolitan society today, ranged from social competition to a true appreciation of aesthetic merit. Most, but by no means all, of these people were likely to be associated with the courts, but there were now a number who came from a very rich class of financiers or bankers, often persons of considerable taste and ingenuity but whose birth denied them direct access to royal circles. This new group is worth noting, since it was something of an extension beyond the old traditional—and usually conservative—interest of burgher town fathers, whose patronage had long existed at this point. If anything, these newer figures were in the tradition of the great Renaissance merchant princes whose support of art had been so important at that time. Their activity was also rather different, both in the quality and scale of its support, from the great middle-class expansion that was to reach flood proportions in the last decades of the century and create a market

of its own, and even a form of society counter to that of the nobility.

In this connection, it is significant that, as late as 1754, Chippendale saw fit to dedicate his *Gentleman and Cabinet Maker's Director*, a voluminous design book-cum-catalogue, to the "Nobility and Gentry" as his clients. Yet, in doing so, he certainly took some liberties with the word "gentleman" as the 18th century would have understood it in the strictest interpretation, to include such persons as the newer type of clients. By the same token, had any leader of the Paris *ébénistes* made out a list of his more rewarding patrons, he would probably have included quite a number of this mixed sort, who were very rich but who would not have been thought worthy of an invitation to Versailles.

An obvious corollary to such a development lay in new attitudes to fashion. The old idea that what was good enough for father was good enough for son now changed for the more advanced coteries, although for many other people such a traditional atavism naturally remained. Among the fashionable a more ephemeral idea took hold, which favored the approach that any rooms might be altered in a year or two and that new creations might come in quick succession. This, of course, accords with our contemporary thought, when in most homes owners think nothing of refurbishing every other year or so, as an affluent consumer society encourages if not dictates.

The new developments came from, and are signaled by, a considerable change in the status and activity of the great English cabinetmakers and Parisian *ébénistes*, who by now were occupied also as dealers and largely led (or at least interpreted) the changes of design and taste. We have noted their advance from the old carpenter-joiner tradition in the century before. By the mid-18th century they had changed again to become persons more nearly akin to our present-day interior decorators, but generally with stock and a shop of their own.

We talk glibly about Chippendale or Cressant, B.V.R.B. (Van Riesenburgh), Riesener, Roentgen, and dozens of others, and most people think of working craftsmen-artists, someone akin to a painter or a sculptor. But—and this is a great "but"—for a true perspective of the situation, it is very much open to question whether any such men, once established as we know of them today, ever themselves did a day's work at the bench.

Though the workshops' founders were no doubt originally practical working apprentices in their youth, once they had advanced to the distinction by which we know them, they had left the workshop floor to become owner-managers of a fairly considerable business and shop operation. They may still have supervised their craftsmen, chosen designs or commissioned them from artists, and built up their stock, but principally it was consulting with clients, getting customers, advising them on their home furnishings and decoration, and all the rest of the poodle-faking that went with any business which had to do with the upper classes that took up most of their time. This point is emphasized by the fact that in both London and Paris a widow might well inherit her husband's business or also by the fact that Sheraton, whose name is credited to thousands of pieces, did not—as far as is known for certain—ever make a piece of furniture with his own hands during his lifetime. In his case he presumably started life in the trade, but his great influence was through his books of designs, carried out between bouts of lay preaching and the like.

Soliciting bad debts was quite a business too, if correspondence of the time can be given credence. As their bills show clearly, the all-embracing nature of their new designer-dealer activity was also a marked feature of the trade. Not only were most furniture-makers of this era prepared to advise on and supply the finest furniture, but they were usually also quite ready to take on the task of doing whole houses, from state rooms to servants' attics. In many cases they also provided for what had once been the upholsterer's province, that is, the soft furnishings, fabrics, wallpaper, and the rest. Formerly these would have been the prerogative of members of other guilds according to the old tradition. Now the "Cabinet Maker" was prepared to arrange the lot, even if he did not stock the actual materials or manufacture them himself. Incidentally, in many cases they were funeral directors as well—hiring out the mourning trappings and taking advantage, as was suggested on some trade cards, of buying up anything the heirs might not have wanted in order to encourage them to order new furnishings.

As the new and widening social concentration with its emphasis on entertainment and display progressed, the elaboration of the background against which to conduct all such socializing advanced. New or improved educational opportunities and amenities also called for further change. New types of rooms and furniture evolved to replace the all-purpose "living hall" or living room which had remained the focus of domestic life since much earlier times.

Certainly, by the later decades of the century, most houses with any claim to being in fashion had a separate special dining room. For the new social encounters a special "withdrawing room" (drawing room) was needed for formal occasions, or a boudoir or morning room for less ceremonious reception. These last chambers took the place of the bedroom, which for the 17th-century hostess had served for receiving daytime guests. Apart from court levees, the bed now served only for sleeping or lovemaking. This trend away from formal utilization of the bedroom had been going on for quite some time, but now it gathered momentum.

As a result of all this, it is little wonder that the period is marked by the expansion of what we may call specialist furniture, pieces designed to provide for one or another aspect of the particular developments in custom we have just touched upon. These remained, of course, an upper- or an upper-middle-class affair.

With the advance of literacy came great advances in printing and publishing and increase in the sale of books. Libraries and bookrooms, or at least bookcases, became an essential for every home with the least claim to being civilized. This counted for even quite modest houses, where a century before a Bible, along with perhaps a book of sermons, would have been the only reading matter—texts which not every member of the house might have been able to decipher. As far as furniture was concerned, formerly the Bible had probably been kept in a "Bible box." Now, the great had a separate library, which called for furniture adapted to the purpose. Other bookrooms had at least special cases for holding their owner's collections of reading matter. Such larger-scale collecting was generally a masculine affair. This showed in the design of the furniture itself, which was solid and comfortable, sturdy reading tables and chairs, set out among library steps, print racks, and built-in cases for the books, which finished off the architectural aspect. Alongside this came an advance in women's reading, especially of novels (which had just come widely into daily life) as also of poetry. For these, little bookcases or wall racks were joined with the writing desk to lend an atmosphere of culture to the boudoir.

The development of the desk or writing table was in itself another reflection of the advance of literacy. Far more people took to writing letters, and as a result writing furniture became a feature of the day. Desks and secrétaires multiplied and certainly gave fruitful inspiration for variations of design. On the

Continent the *bureau plat,* in various forms, found a favored place. Since women tended to engage in this social letter writing more than men, so-called ladies' desks evolved in special profusion. Because, for the most part, these pieces were called upon to serve for little more than occasional effusions which helped to fill an otherwise quite trivial day, many were of proportions and an unsteadiness that would drive any busy modern woman mad. Nonetheless, this did not stop them from often being very pretty pieces, and by the end of the century they had become an essential feature of room decoration.

One of the most lasting significant innovations of this time lay in the establishment of separate dining or "eating" rooms, in which by mid-century permanent tables had replaced the previous trestle tables of general utility. These quickly evolved such special features as extension leaves and central supports, which made for greater freedom of the diners' legs—especially when drunk. Accompanying the dining tables were sets of matching chairs, which served to make a nice effect when everything was set in place in the room. These had to be substantial enough to contain the fidgeting of tipsy men when the women had withdrawn to take tea, with the resulting logical effects on design, as on upholstery.

Sideboards followed, first rather as a development from earlier buffets, which had served mainly for the display of tableware and sometimes of liquor and wine. As the habit of passing separate courses grew (though not until quite late), so the sideboard had its function of providing somewhere to set the meats and other dishes as they came out of the kitchen and between servings. For a hundred years the dining room, so evolved, became not only a convenience to avoid the odors and debris of food preparation and eating but also a status feature of the prosperous 19th-century household—and still remains so. Once again it is on the decline, since lack of serving help and increasing cost, especially in urban areas, now encourages a less extravagant use of the necessary space.

The withdrawing, or drawing, rooms which became the center of most other domestic entertainment, whether gambling or conversation, also became the setting for all the finest cabinets, display pieces, and other furnishings. Drawing room chairs were of the most refined type, the upholstery and drapes of the finest silks and damasks, or tapestry and embroidery. The tables and cabinets or chests were as fine as means and money could make them. For a generation which did not believe in hiding any social consequence or material advantage, these developments were not surprising.

Although no longer public rooms, bedrooms usually took on a rather formal air, in which for persons of taste fine cupboards and chests of drawers replaced the wall closet—more often perhaps as contributing to the general elegance rather than for showing off possessions. Elaborate toilet tables could enhance the bedroom's last contribution before going on to less intimate affairs. There was often attendance at the dressing ceremonies, which was a custom that, as was suggested earlier, might have been inherited from royal practice. If ladyships no longer received and showed themselves grandly arranged in their beds, they did admit intimates to watch them being frizzed and permed, patched, powdered, and made up. Men too might receive their gossips in this way, while preening in private.

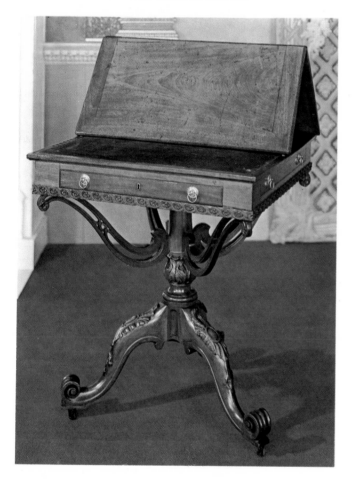

265 Reading table, with folding top and
carved tripod base. English, 1770; made by
William France for Kenwood House.
Victoria and Albert Museum, London.

266 Mahogany organ case. English, similar to a
design (dated 1760) that appeared in later
edition of Chippendale's *Director*.
Victoria and Albert Museum, London.

268 *(above)* Mahogany two-tier table (dumbwaiter) on tripod feet. English, mid-18th century. Victoria and Albert Museum, London.

267 *(above)* Magohany wardrobe, with drawers below. English, 1760. Victoria and Albert Museum, London.

269 *(right)* Mahogany tea table, with claw-and-ball feet and pierced edging. English, c. 1750. Victoria and Albert Museum, London.

270 Mahogany breakfast table, with openwork "Chinese paling" panels and doors around lower shelf. English, c. 1755; similar to design in Chippendale's *Gentleman and Cabinet Maker's Director* (1754). Victoria and Albert Museum, London.

163

271 (above) Mahogany china cabinet, carved in Chinese taste. English, c. 1760. This "China case," as the type was designated in Chippendale's *Director*, once belonged to Queen Victoria's father. B. Vangelisti Collection, Lucca.

272 Mahogany chair, carved with *chinoiserie* fantasy. English, mid-18th century. Elaborately carved furniture such as this shows the felicitous encounter of the so-called "Chinese taste" with rococo style. Lady Lever Art Gallery, Port Sunlight (Cheshire).

273 *(below)* Mahogany display cabinet, designed in Gothic Revival taste. English, c. 1760–70. Victoria and Albert Museum, London.

274 *(right)* Mahogany display cabinet in Chinese taste. English, third quarter of 18th century. This piece was constructed to contain a smaller Oriental cabinet of tortoise shell and ivory. Victoria and Albert Museum, London (formerly at Claydon House, Buckinghamshire).

165

275 *(above)* Japanned commode, with gilt *chinoiserie* on black ground (originally red). English, c. 1755. Victoria and Albert Museum, London (formerly in the Chinese Bedroom at Badminton House, Gloucestershire).

276 *(left)* Armchair of carved and gilded wood, in "French taste." English, c. 1750. The varied decoration of the legs and armrests suggests that this piece was a chairmaker's display sample. Victoria and Albert Museum, London.

277 Bed in Chinese taste of carved pine,
japanned in red, black, and gold (with modern
curtains). English, c. 1755. This lavish piece
from the Chinese Bedroom at Badminton House
(Gloucestershire) is attributed to either
Chippendale or William Linnell.
Victoria and Albert Museum, London.

278 *(left)* Mahogany chair in Chinese taste. English, c. 1760; based on a design in Chippendale's *Director*. Victoria and Albert Museum, London.

279 *(below)* Mahogany settee in Chinese taste, with triple-chair backrest. English, 1750–60. Victoria and Albert Museum, London.

280 *(below)* Lacquer cabinet in Chinese taste.
English, c. 1755; perhaps by Chippendale.
Victoria and Albert Museum, London
(formerly in Badminton House).

281 *(right)* "Ribband-back" chair of carved
mahogany. English, mid-18th century; after a
design in the first edition of Chippendale's
Director (1754). Victoria and Albert Museum,
London.

282 *(right)* Mahogany armchair in Gothic Revival
taste. English, third quarter of 18th century.
Victoria and Albert Museum, London.

169

283 *(above)* Council Room in Webb House,
Wethersfield, Connecticut. American, 1752.
Here, in 1781, General George Washington and
Count de Rochambeau, with their aides,
planned the historic Yorktown Campaign.
(Photo: Louis H. Frohman)

284 *(right)* Mahogany highboy. American
(Philadelphia), c. 1770. Henry Francis du Pont
Winterthur Museum, Wilmington, Delaware.

285 *(far right)* Blackwell Parlor, from house on
Pine Street, Philadelphia. American, mid-18th
century. The richly carved fireplace frame and
the Philadelphia furniture are among the finest
examples of pre-Revolutionary American
craftsmanship. The "sample" wing chair is
attributed to Benjamin Randolph; the
cut-glass chandelier is Irish. Henry Francis
du Pont Winterthur Museum, Wilmington,
Delaware.

286 *(below)* Charleston Dining Room, from house on Broad Street in Charleston, South Carolina. American, 1772; built for William Burrows, a lawyer and judge. The Massachusetts dining table is surrounded by twelve walnut chairs of simple Rhode Island type. The English cut-glass chandelier dates from about 1760. Henry Francis du Pont Winterthur Museum, Wilmington, Delaware.

287 Port Royal Parlor, with woodwork from
Edward Stiles' house at Frankford, near
Philadelphia. The fireplace is flanked by an
impressive pair of Philadelphia sofas with
cabriole legs and claw-and-ball feet, once
owned by John Dickinson, author of *Letters
from a Farmer in Pennsylvania* (1768). The
Philadelphia mahogany highboy in the
background is shown in close-up (*284*).
The cut-glass candelabra and the
glass-and-ormolu chandelier are English.
Henry Francis du Pont Winterthur Museum,
Wilmington, Delaware.

288 *(above)* Walnut-veneer table, with carved walnut legs and inlaid top. Austrian, mid-18th century. Harrach Gallery, Vienna. (Photo: Meyer)

289 *(right)* Bureau writing table, with rosewood and tulipwood veneer and ivory inlay. Italian (Piedmont), c. 1760; by Pietro Piffetti. Palazzina di Caccia, Stupinigi.

290 Room from Donndorf, near Bayreuth, paneled
and floored in parquetry of contrasting natural
and stained woods. German, after 1758;
constructed by the Spindler brothers. The
commode, probably of slightly later date, was
designed for this room by the same craftsmen.
The inlaid chair is by Abraham Roentgen of
Neuwied. Bayerisches Nationalmuseum, Munich.

291 Bureau-cabinet, with classical scenes in French
taste. German (Silesia), 1775; signed and dated
by J. C. Fiedler. Among the scenes is one
depicting Frederick the Great in the guise of a
Roman emperor. Museum für Kunst und
Gewerbe, Hamburg. (Photo: Kleinhempel)

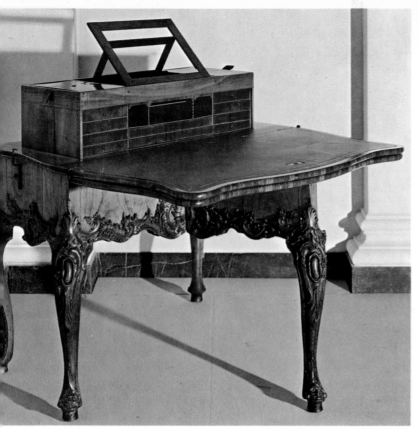

292 *(above)* Fruitwood "harlequin" card and writing table, with two flaps supported by a gate-leg and with a rising rack of drawers. German, 1750–60; by Abraham Roentgen of Neuwied. Victoria and Albert Museum, London.

293 *(left)* "Harlequin" card and writing table, with three hinged flaps fitted for different games; with checkered veneer of ivory, mother-of-pearl, and bronze and with gilt-bronze mounts. German, c. 1765; made by Abraham Roentgen of Neuwied for the Elector of Trier. Museum für Kunsthandwerk, Frankfurt.

294 *(above)* Bureau with pictorial marquetry of decorative woods, ivory, and mother-of-pearl and with gilt-bronze mounts. German, c. 1765; made by Abraham and David Roentgen for the Elector of Trier. Rijksmuseum, Amsterdam.

295 Medal cabinet, veneered with cedar and
mounted with gilt metal. German, 1775; made
by Tüllmann for the collection of gems and
medals of Frederick the Great. Schloss
Charlottenburg, Berlin.

296 *(below)* Double-sided writing desk, veneered
with walnut and mahogany. German, 1765–70;
made by Balthasar Hermann for the
Prince-Bishop of Bamberg, Adam Friedrich
von Seinsheim, whose monogram appears in the
gilt cartouches. The desk may be used from
either side, depending on which way the top is
rolled back. Neue Residenz, Bamberg.
(Photo: Bauer)

297 Mirrored writing bureau, veneered with burr
walnut and inlaid with palisander and rosewood.
Italian (Piedmont), mid-18th century.
Palazzina di Caccia, Stupinigi.

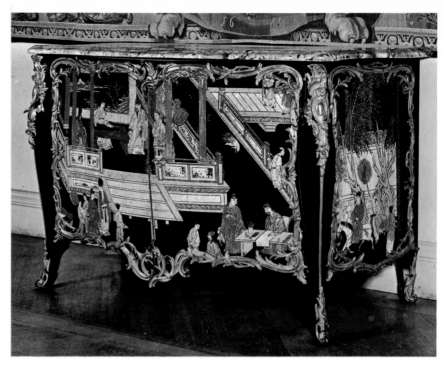

298 *(below)* Console-commode, with panels of Japanese lacquer, ormolu mounts, and marble top. French, mid-18th century (Louis XV period); by Bernard van Riesenburgh. Mr. and Mrs. Charles B. Wrightsman Collection, New York.

299 *(above)* Commode, covered with Chinese coromandel lacquer within rococo ormolu borders. French, mid-18th century (Louis XV period); by Carel. Louvre, Paris (formerly at Château de Valençay, Loire; cliché des Musées Nationaux).

300 Marquetry writing table (*bureau plat*), with ormolu mounts and inlaid with flowers in various woods. French, third quarter of 18th century (late Louis XV period); by Jean François Oeben. Residenzmuseum, Munich.

301 *(left)* Secrétaire, with floral marquetry in various woods, ormolu mounts, and marble top. French, c. 1760; by Jean François Oeben. Residenzmuseum, Munich.

302 *(below)* Commode, veneered with lacquer panels and mounted with rococo ormolu borders. French, third quarter of 18th century (Louis XV period); by Jean Demoulin. Musée des Beaux-Arts, Tours (formerly at Château de Chanteloup).

303 Commode, with ormolu mounts and marquetry panel framed by ormolu laurel branches. French, late 18th century (Louis XVI period); by Jean Henri Riesener. Musée des Arts Décoratifs, Paris.

304 *(below)* Commode, with five drawers and breakfront central marquetry panel of still-life subject. French, c. 1765 (Transitional period); by Pierre Roussel. Musée Jacquemart-André, Paris.

305 *(right)* Long-case pendulum clock of tulipwood and kingwood, with ormolu mounts and sunflower motif. French, c. 1770; by Nicolas Petit. The clockworks are signed by Lepaute; a more or less identical piece is also found in Buckingham Palace. Conservatoire des Arts et Métiers, Paris.

306 *(right)* Two-drawer commode, with tulipwood and kingwood veneer and ormolu mounts. French, 1774 (Transitional period); by Gilles Joubert. Victoria and Albert Museum, London (once in the apartments of Madame Adelaide, daughter of Louis XV, in the Château de Marly).

307 *(right)* Clothes chest, with eighteen small drawers and with tambour shutters veneered in cube parquetry. This piece forms the pair to an upright *secrétaire à abattant*. French, c. 1760; by Jean François Oeben.

308 Mahogany commode, with gilt-bronze mounts and marquetry doors of varied woods. English, c. 1770; attributed to John Cobb. Victoria and Albert Museum, London.

309 *(below)* Commode with veneer of various woods and gilt-bronze mounts. Italian (Naples), mid-18th century. Museo Correale, Sorrento.

310 Veneered commode, with six drawers, side cupboards, and gilt-bronze mounts. English, c. 1770; possibly made by Thomas Chippendale. Manchester City Art Galleries (England).

311 (right) Bombé-commode, with gilt-bronze mounts and marquetry in stained and rare woods. English, c. 1770–75; probably by an immigrant craftsman from the Continent. Victoria and Albert Museum, London (formerly at Hagley Park, Worcestershire).

312 (right) Mahogany *secrétaire à abattant*, with Sèvres porcelain plaques and ormolu floral arabesques. French, porcelains dated 1773; by Martin Carlin. Metropolitan Museum of Art, New York (gift of Samuel H. Kress Foundation).

313 (below) Commode of mahogany and ebony, with porcelain plaques and ormolu ornament. French, late 18th century (Louis XVI period); made by Adam Weisweiler. This piece was sold to King George IV. (Reproduced by gracious permission of Her Majesty Queen Elizabeth II)

186

314 *(above)* Commode, with marble top and large
panels of Sèvres porcelain secured by an ormolu
trellis. French, porcelain dated 1758–60; by
Bernard van Riesenburgh. Private collection.

315 *(right)* Worktable of painted wood, with
Sèvres porcelain top and ormolu mounts.
French, porcelain dated 1766; signed "BVRB"
(Bernard van Riesenburgh). Louvre, Paris
(cliché des Musées Nationaux).

317 *(right)* Long-case clock of tulipwood and kingwood, with ormolu mounts, topped by an allegorical bronze figure of Time. French, late 18th century (Louis XVI period). The case is by Balthazar Lieutaud; clockworks are signed "Robin à Paris." Wallace Collection, London.

316 Console sideboard (*commode-desserte*), with mahogany and satinwood veneer and ormolu mounts. French, late 18th century (Louis XVI period); by Martin Carlin. Musée Nissim de Camondo, Paris.

318 *(above)* Ebony-veneer writing table, with panels of Japanese lacquer and ormolu legs and mounts. French, late 18th century; designed by Adam Weisweiler, with ormolu fittings attributed to Pierre Gouthière. It is known to have been intended, in 1784, for use by Marie-Antoinette at the Château de Saint-Cloud. Louvre, Paris.

319 *(right)* Harpsichord *(clavecin)* in a japanned case *(vernis Martin)*, set on a carved gilt stand. French, 1786. Signed and dated by the celebrated harpsichordmaker Pascal Taskin, this instrument is of unusually small size. Victoria and Albert Museum, London.

320 Mahogany *bureau plat*, with ormolu mounts. French, 1787; made by Guillaume Beneman for the library of Louis XVI at Fontainebleau. Louvre, Paris.

189

321-322 *(left and below)* Library table and chair, veneered with burr walnut and inlaid in light and dark woods. Bohemian, mid-18th century. With its backrest folded in, the chair fits into the kneehole; the table also unfolds and doubles over to serve as library steps. Museum of Czechoslovak Literature, Prague.

323 *(right)* Philosophy Room from the Convent of Strahow, in Prague. Bohemian, end of 18th century. The bookcases are of pale fruitwood with lavish gilt ornaments. Built at the close of the 18th century, under a decorative painted ceiling by Anton Maulbertsch (1724-96), this imposing library shows the persistence of rococo style. Museum of Czechoslovak Literature, Prague.

324 Library at Kenwood House, near London.
English, 1767–69 (date of original drawings,
now in Soane Museum); designed by Robert
Adam. Painted in contrasting colors and gilded,
the stuccowork by Joseph Rose contains
neoclassical paintings by Antonio Zucchi.
The various seating furniture was designed for
Spencer House, about 1760, by the architect
James Stuart. (Courtesy of Greater London
Council as Trustees of the Iveagh Bequest,
Kenwood)

The Late 18th Century

(Plates 324–383)

This section is concerned mainly with those fashions which flourished during the second half of the 18th century and which arose out of new classical interests fostered by excavations and studies conducted by international dilettantes. Though quickly followed by others, the leading protagonists were mainly from London or Paris, and it is fitting that the opening illustrations for this period (pp. 192, 197–201) should record the work of Robert Adam. The first (Plate 324), showing an entire room, serves to emphasize the essentially wholesale quality of the movement, embracing architecture and decorative schemes as well as individual pieces of furniture. Though the ideas were not entirely new, the results were very fine in the case of Adam, in whose ideal everything was envisaged as part of a whole complex. Every detail, from walls and ceiling to doorknobs, was designed by the architect himself.

Naturally, such extreme refinement was not to everybody's taste or purse. As with all such movements the ideas and novelties of the classicists were quickly borrowed and incorporated into designs bearing the stamp of earlier traditions. This was true both for England and the United States (pp. 202–203), and even for certain Continental areas where rococo tended to persist (pp. 204–205).

In France the styles overlapped, and although the 1770s could display Versailles-type pieces or Louis XV rococo still in production, the new fashion was enthusiastically taken up both by a group at court and by sufficiently wealthy persons outside court circles (pp. 206–209).

In some places the influence of the simple English mahogany taste was associated with classical decorative motifs in ormolu mounts to create the essentials of what came to be called Empire (pp. 210–211). In Italy and Spain, the rather later manifestations tend to be fuller and richer, bearing witness to their baroque-rococo ancestry (pp. 212–217, 220–223). The remaining plates in this section show how other Continental areas such as Germany and Holland generally continued in a more traditional taste in this period.

Although each generation's way of life and furnishings would seem to reflect the general circumstances of the period in which it lived, the decades around 1800 were perhaps among the most clearly marked in all history in this respect. If nothing else, it is remarkable how the strong interest in ancient classical forms could be adapted first for monarchy, then revolutionary movements, and finally empire.

That traditional lines of design should continue to parallel this development was no more unnatural than at any other time, but that a new middle-class market should spring up with a style of its own—not merely a provincial dilution or reduction—and run concurrently with both as a third fashionable line was something of a novelty. This is really what was happening in the third and fourth quarters of the 18th century. The stress was still on France and England, the former perhaps for more traditional persistences—at least up till the Revolution—and England for new developments which were at first restricted to the English-speaking world but which were to spread in influence, especially where political alignment might make the taste acceptable on intellectual as well as decorating grounds.

The neoclassic as it began was fairly evenly, and mainly, distributed between France and England. The first evidences began to appear shortly after the middle of the 18th century, as an offshoot of upper-class interest in archeological studies and excavations then being done at Pompeii and Herculaneum and researches at classical sites in the Near East. This was but another reflection of the domination of upper-class education by classical history and literature. At the outset, whether in England or France, the movement was limited to a small intellectual coterie of the very rich. However, the mingling of influences between London and Paris was facilitated since both craftsmen and patrons traveled regularly.

In England the spread of the new style owed much to the drawings and studies of the architect Robert Adam, who was commissioned to realize his designs by at least two magnificent patrons very soon after his return from the Grand Tour. Equally generous encouragement both from the court—including from Marie-Antoinette and some princes—and from great financiers enabled French designers also to have their way on an ambitious scale in the neoclassic vein.

If there is any difference between the two streams, it may be that Adam's archeological efforts produced a rather more serious approach, whereas the influence of the French queen and her entourage may—but only *may*—have been responsible for the lighter handling and rather fussier, gayer, and more decorative adaptations made in France under the monarchy. On the whole, however, it was the evolution influenced by the Revolution that was to be more widely effective for the following generations. Full neoclassicism, which was destined to become more a deliberate reflection of political attitudes than a cultivated gentleman's hobby, will be looked at in the next section.

The changes which took place in more traditional design were fairly natural reactions on both sides of the Channel and again reflect in reasonable measure the society for which they were created. In France an increasingly more detached, court-oriented group followed the queen and other aristocrats into a make-believe world that none ever thought would tumble down around their heads, still less that their own heads would tumble with its loss. So they went their way surrounded by ever-greater luxury, more and more contrived and precious as it sought novelty.

The alternative reactions to the older styles that were becoming stale would have been either a return to full pomposity—as was to come later in the 19th century—or an even greater lightening of the Louis XV reactions. The compromise may have done something of the latter sort, but a wholehearted move to simplicity was not in accord with the artificial setup of the Versailles court to which the entire society, or at least the tastemaking segment of it, had become accustomed. It almost seemed as if this dominant group were so rigidly set in their Versailles ways that they could not envisage change, and so some degree of compromise prevailed.

The invention of the mid-century seemed dried up, and as if for sheer novelty its place was taken by an almost onanistic, aging urgency toward fussy and intricate minutiae of decoration, whether in carving, painting, or ormolu work. Even many of the neoclassic introductions were diluted by being subjected to this tendency. A nymph or goddess of a reasonable Pompeian ancestry was so garlanded with wreaths and flowers, chains and chiseling, until reduced like some abstract filigree to just an ingenious display of fine technique. Admittedly, this was perhaps most characteristic of the highest court conceits, and other patrons, who now included many from the world of trade and finance, still patronized leading *ébénistes* for less-exaggerated pieces which maintained the old tradition of fine design and workmanship, enriched with ormolu and marquetry, but which were relieved of the curves and excesses of the previous decades. For such clients of traditional orientation, the members of chairs, tables, commodes, and cabinets might be further refined, but held to basic principles. Devices for enriching decorative fantasy, such as the lacquer that had always been resorted to, were still in vogue, and other novelties such as high-grade metal plaques or porcelains were introduced for greater effect. One hesitates to use such an abused, subjective word as "decadent" for any art, but sometimes attitudes of such obvious exaggeration do seem the efforts of a tired society, however pretty the end result may be. Alliteration apart, rococo was robuster in its way.

Elsewhere on the Continent the baroque-rococo was slow to die, and although certain innovations had effect, both on traditional and newer styles, by straightening out line and calling for greater purity, it was not until a later generation that the literally clean sweep of neoclassic dictates would lead to that greater austerity, and even severity, we usually associate with them.

Horace Walpole, who disliked the manifestations of this trend in England, could refer to Adam's bed at Osterley Park as "snippets of gingerbread." His term could well be applied to many Paris pieces of the time, as the illustrations show. Although the influence of Greco-Roman studies made its point in design, this work is probably best considered as a modification of the 18th-century stylistic course, and hence is classed as such here.

In England, besides the work of Adam or the intellectual diversion of revolutionary sympathizers, an all-important force was moving to create another type of revolution within the business of furniture and furnishings itself. We noted in the last section that what the English call the Industrial Revolution had created great new wealth, as had a regular expansion in foreign trade, and that the significant point of this was that the monetary proceeds were spread not only among a small privileged group but a sizable new middle group of gentry and lesser bourgeoisie as well. Like the misses of Miss Austen or the mammas of hundreds of earlier novels filling the library shelves, they saw themselves in their own mirrors as not all that removed from those who led the fashion. Novelists and popular printmakers may have caricatured them, and the stage rocked with laughter at their antics as they pretended to the manners of their betters, but as big frogs in small ponds they cut such figure as they could. They decked out their parlors and drawing rooms with chairs and tables, carpets, trinkets, drapes, and other furnishings, and even with pianofortes and harps, which bespoke their new pretension.

This movement had been going on everywhere to some degree, but was especially marked in England, where the social picture gave a greater chance to those who wished to climb. The trickle quite soon became a flood as manors and burghers' houses and even yeomen's farms were furnished in such an imitation of the ruling fashion as purses would allow. This led to something of a mixture in the shops. On the one side was the fashionable market, with its classical emphasis handed down from Adam and also influenced by French taste. But other designers—in England, for example, Sheraton and, less perhaps, Hepplewhite—also catered to the traditional English taste for simplicity, adapting it to new needs in creating the styles which bear their names.

The results are immediately apparent and often very pretty, yet also often pretentious in a curious way. This is the furniture for a new ostentatious society; it is delicate, but also "refined" and "genteel," with the best and worst connotations of these words.

Except where the forms were specifically masculine, as in dining rooms and libraries designed for men, the spindle legs and the delicate, fragile workboxes, minute desks, occasional tables, and all the rest were scarcely practical pieces to live with for any reasonably straightforward person, whether male or female. Production to satisfy the taste of the now successful middle class was made with every shade of gentility that pretension could demand. This movement to "refeened" gentility would not seem far removed from some Scandinavian modern pieces which have been so popular in recent decades and which in their way derive from Sheraton or Hepplewhite.

To cope with all this change and growth, many cabinetmakers were on the way to almost becoming large-scale furniture manufacturers to cater to the new demands. While some retained their exclusivity, others who were perhaps more businesslike or less aesthetic sought wider fields, and from the type of development we saw in early Chippendale a new and ever more ambitious tendency evolved.

Similar to the traditional continuity in France, there was in England much conservative design that ran alongside all the novelties, above all in the simple mahogany work we usually call Chippendale. This essentially English (or, perhaps, in view of its continuation in the New World, we should say "English-speaking") taste still accounted for a great proportion of the ordinary work. Here we must necessarily concentrate more on the finer pieces. A firm like Gillow accommodated exclusive if old-fashioned clients ordering "Mr. Chippendale's chest" ritually every year from scanning designs published in the *Director*. Although right at the end of the century the mahogany tradition was adjusting to the trend of the times—for example, turned instead of square-type legs and flatter backs instead of splat—its purveyors until about 1800 were still reluctant to adopt the neoclassic ways of Thomas Hope. Even then the change was not a step toward modernization but was attributable to the fact that overwhelming innovations of Napoleon were then on their way to alter the attitudes of three-quarters of the continent whose map the Corsican ruler was to change so drastically in 1806.

325 Gilded side table designed for the Tapestry Room at Osterley Park, with painted frieze panels, marble top, and polychrome inlay. English, 1775; designed by Robert Adam. Osterley Park, Middlesex.

326 (below) Sideboard table with mahogany top and gilded carved frieze and legs. English, 1767; made by John Linnell according to a design by Robert Adam. Osterley Park, Middlesex.

327 *(right)* Marquetry commode, with neoclassic hardwood and satinwood inlay; mouldings mounted with gilt metal. English, c. 1770; probably designed by Robert Adam. Osterley Park, Middlesex.

328 *(below)* Display cabinet, with veneer and inlay of rosewood and satinwood and gilt-bronze mounts. English, 1771; designed by Robert Adam. This piece was made for Kimbolton Castle (Huntingdonshire) to show to advantage eleven Italian scenic panels in *pietre dure*, which are signed and dated 1709 by Baccio Capelli (Florence). Victoria and Albert Museum, London.

329 *(above)* State bed of carved wood, painted and gilded; hung with velvet curtains and a silk-lined interior. English, 1776; designed for this room by Robert Adam. The fireplace, mantel mirror, armchair, and firescreen are all probably Adam designs as well. Osterley Park, Middlesex.

330 *(right)* Pier glass and marble-topped side table of gilded wood, English, c. 1777; designed as a unit by Robert Adam. Osterley Park, Middlesex.

331 So-called "Etruscan Room" at Osterley Park,
Middlesex. English, 1775–77 (designs); by
Robert Adam. This simple, handsome interior
exemplifies the "Etruscan style" introduced
into England by Adam about 1770. Inspired by
classical wall paintings, this harmonious
decorative scheme might be compared for its
imaginative beauty to some of the architectonic
inventions of Piranesi.

333 Shield-back armchair of painted satinwood. English, c. 1790. This design is associated with the firm of George Seddon. Victoria and Albert Museum, London.

332 (below) Mahogany dining chair with lyre back and fluted frame. English, 1767; designed by Robert Adam and made by John Linnell. Osterley Park, Middlesex.

334 Chair of carved and gilded wood. English, c. 1795; designed by Henry Holland for the Prince of Wales' residence (later King George IV) at Carlton House. Victoria and Albert Museum, London (lent by Her Majesty Queen Elizabeth II).

335 *(above)* Lyre-back armchair of inlaid rosewood with gilt-metal mounts and medallion. English, c. 1770; made by John Linnell from an Adam design. Osterley Park, Middlesex.

336 *(right)* Cylinder bureau-bookcase of satinwood, with inlaid linear designs and rosewood panels. English, c. 1790; similar to models of Hepplewhite and Sheraton of slightly earlier date. Victoria and Albert Museum, London.

337 *(left)* Mahogany dressing table on cabriole legs, with hardwood panels inlaid with different woods in neoclassic motifs. English, c. 1770–75. Victoria and Albert Museum, London.

338 *(below)* So-called "Library Cross Hall." American, in style of c. 1800. The walls are covered with a French scenic *papier peint.* The long-case clock, dating from about the decades 1790–1810, is signed by Simon Willard. The small writing table and the chairs are Boston-made pieces of about the same date. Henry Francis du Pont Winterthur Museum, Wilmington, Delaware.

339 Salon furnished with mainly Portuguese
neoclassic pieces. Spanish-Portuguese, c. 1800.
The lower parts of the walls are covered with
gaily colored ceramic murals (*azulejos*) of
figural and floral motifs— a type of decoration
that was used even in the most elegant Iberian
interiors of the period. Fundaçao R. do Espirito
Santo Silva, Lisbon.

340 *(below)* Side chair of carved and painted wood. Italian (Lucca), 1765; signed by its maker, Angelo Colognari di Castiglione di Lucca. Bottega di San Giusto, Lucca.

341 *(above)* Carved writing table and cabinet of painted and gilded wood, with small drawers and open-back shelves. Italian (Ferrara?), first half of 18th century. Casa Serristori, Florence.

342 *(left)* A corner of Marie-Antoinette's Cabinet de Méridienne, in the Palace of Versailles. French, late 18th century. The paneling, carved by the Rousseau brothers, dates from 1781. The table is a rare example of metal furniture, usually made for court use in this period. The gilded chair may have been made for the Comte d'Artois, brother of Louis XVI, and the modern Lyons silks are a restoration in the style of the period.

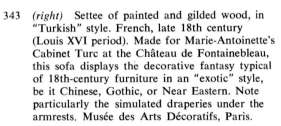

343 *(right)* Settee of painted and gilded wood, in "Turkish" style. French, late 18th century (Louis XVI period). Made for Marie-Antoinette's Cabinet Turc at the Château de Fontainebleau, this sofa displays the decorative fantasy typical of 18th-century furniture in an "exotic" style, be it Chinese, Gothic, or Near Eastern. Note particularly the simulated draperies under the armrests. Musée des Arts Décoratifs, Paris.

344 *(left)* Cylinder bureau, with mother-of-pearl veneer held by a steel trellis and ormolu mounts. French, c. 1784–87; made by Jean Henri Riesener for Marie-Antoinette's boudoir at Fontainebleau. The combination of materials delicately used here is extremely rare. Château de Fontainebleau.

345 *(right)* Marie-Antoinette's boudoir, Château de Fontainebleau. French, late 18th century (1787?). The paneling is painted in the neoclassic Pompeian taste, probably by the Rousseau brothers. The worktable is by Jean Henri Riesener, and the sculptural piece above the doorway perhaps by Dauphin de Beauvais.

346 *(above)* Grand Salon, Musée Nissim de Camondo, Paris. French, mainly late 18th century. The matching commodes alongside the fireplace are signed by Adam Weisweiler; the small Sèvres-topped writing table is by Martin Carlin. The needlework-upholstered divan, chairs, and firescreen are by Georges Jacob, and the desk chair is attributed to J. R. Nadal.

347 *(far left)* Gilded wooden armchair, with curved tapering back. French, 1787; made by Jean Baptiste Claude Sené for the *cabinet* of Marie-Antoinette at Saint-Cloud. Louvre, Paris (cliché des Musées Nationaux).

348 *(left)* Side chairs of painted and gilded wood. French, c. 1770; by Louis Delanois. Similar chairs were made for Madame du Barry about the same time. López-Willshaw Collection, Neuilly-sur-Seine.

349 *(right)* Reconstruction of an interior of the Louis XVI period. French, late 18th century. The paneling, painted grey and blue, is from the Hôtel de Breteuil in Paris. The settee, chair, and circular table are neoclassic designs of the period. Musée Carnavalet, Paris.

350 *(above)* Secrétaire with mahogany veneer and ormolu mounts. German, c. 1800; attributed to David Hacker, but mounts perhaps by David Roentgen. Staatliche Museen Preussischer Kulturbesitz, Kunstgewerbemuseum, Berlin.

351 *(right)* Cylinder bureau, with dark-figured mahogany veneer and ormolu mounts. German, late 18th century. This neoclassic design has a very architectonic effect in its severe geometric lines and the simple ormolu motifs emphasizing them. Baron de Rédé Collection, Paris.

352 *(left)* Mahogany cylinder bureau with ormolu mounts. French, late 18th century (Louis XVI period); by Jean Henri Riesener. The elegant simplicity of this piece, adorned only with ormolu drawer pulls and keyplates, is especially notable for this period. Musée des Arts Décoratifs, Paris.

353 *(below)* Cylinder bureau, with figured mahogany veneer and ormolu mounts. French, c. 1775–85 (Louis XVI period); by Claude Charles Saunier. The restrained ormolu borders are particularly attractive here. Musée Nissim de Camondo, Paris.

354 *(above)* Side table of carved and gilded wood. Italian (Rome), 1769; designed by Giambattista Piranesi. This piece was made for Cardinal Rezzonico in the same year that Piranesi published his *Diverse maniere d'adornare i cammini*, which was to have significant influence on later neoclassic interior design. Minneapolis Institute of Arts.

355 *(below)* Carved wooden side table, with painted floral decoration and gilt ornaments. Italian (Rome), c. 1780. Galleria Borghese, Rome.

356 *(right)* Salone d'Oro in Palazzo Chigi, Rome. Italian, decorated 1765–67. The rich ornament of this fine early neoclassic interior includes the stucco female figures of the doorway lunette by Tommaso Righi.

357 *(left)* Settee of painted wood, with some of the original *chinoiserie* scenic fabric. Italian (Piedmont), c. 1790. Valperga di Masino Collection, Castello di Masino.

358 *(below)* Chest of drawers of painted and gilded wood. Italian (Piedmont), c. 1780–90; perhaps made by Giuseppe Maria Bonzanigo. The generous gold-gilt ornament is in Louis XVI style; the caplike element atop the legs is a singular feature. Palazzo Reale, Turin.

359 Bedroom in the Castello di Masino. Italian (Piedmont), c. 1790. The neoclassic decoration of the imposing bed and the other furniture in this room includes such exotic motifs as carved harpies and animal protomes.

360 *(right)* Lyre-back chair and carved side table, painted and gilded. Italian (Naples), late 18th century. The rich gilt garlands and the spiral legs are notable decorative elements here. Museo Correale, Sorrento.

361 *(below)* Settee and armchair, with painted panels of figures inspired by recently rediscovered Pompeian wall paintings. Italian (Naples), c. 1780. The paired front legs of both the chair and settee are extremely rare. Museo di Capodimonte, Naples.

362 (above) Daybed of carved and painted wood, combining the Chinese and neoclassic tastes. Italian (Lombardy), c. 1780; from Villa Silva at Cinisello Balsamo, near Monza. Both this sofa and the table below are rather extravagant Italian variants of *chinoiserie*, which were created when the Villa Silva was refurnished in this style in the late 18th century. Private collection, Genoa.

363 (below) Side table of carved and painted wood, showing a combination of the Chinese and neoclassic tastes. Italian (Lombardy), c. 1780; from Villa Silva at Cinisello Balsamo, near Monza. Private collection, Turin.

364 *(below)* Carved walnut commode. German (Rhine district), c. 1775–80. Museum für Kunsthandwerk, Frankfurt.

365 *(right)* Wooden armchair with cane seat and scenic motifs painted on a cream ground in the Chinese taste. German, late 18th century. Schloss von Pfaueninsel, Berlin.

366 Armchair of carved and painted wood. English, c. 1790. The backrest decoration bears the device of the Prince of Wales. Victoria and Albert Museum, London.

367 Room with neoclassic painted wall and ceiling
patterns, from Schloss Tattenbach, Munich.
German, c. 1775; designed by François
Cuvilliés (the younger). The ceiling is painted
as an open pergola covered with vines and
flowers; the wall panels contain delicate floral
paintings on silk by Joseph Zächenberger,
noted for his porcelain painting. Bayerisches
Nationalmuseum, Munich.

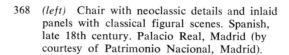

368 *(left)* Chair with neoclassic details and inlaid panels with classical figural scenes. Spanish, late 18th century. Palacio Real, Madrid (by courtesy of Patrimonio Nacional, Madrid).

369 *(below)* Marquetry commode, inlaid with ivory and rare woods. Spanish, late 18th century. Palacio Real, Madrid (by courtesy of Patrimonio Nacional, Madrid).

370 *(left)* Cradle of painted and gilded wood. Italian, c. 1780. Valperga di Masino Collection, Castello di Masino.

371 Bedroom of Queen Maria Luisa, wife of
Carlos IV. Spanish, late 18th century. The walls
and the bed frame are painted and gilded in
the so-called "Pompeian" style of decoration
then current. Palacio Real, Madrid (by courtesy
of Patrimonio Nacional, Madrid).

372 *(below)* Writing table, inlaid with various woods. Italian (Lombardy), c. 1780–90; by Giuseppe Maggiolini. The designs for the marquetry panels were supplied by Giuseppe Levati, a specialist in this style. Private collection, Milan.

373 *(right)* Commode in two parts, with marquetry panels of tulipwood, maple, and mahogany set within a walnut ground. Italian (Lombardy), c. 1780; inlays by Giuseppe Maggiolini, following designs by Andrea Appiani. Civiche Raccolte Artistiche, Milan.

374 *(right)* Chest of drawers, with *chinoiserie* marquetry panels and mounts. Italian (Lombardy), c. 1765; probably by Giuseppe Maggiolini. The marquetry is patterned after designs by Giuseppe Levati. Museo del Castello, Milan.

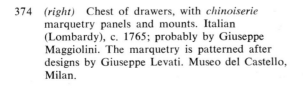

375 *(below)* Jewel casket, bearing pharmaceutical symbols probably denoting the ownership. Italian (Lombardy), c. 1800; signed by Giuseppe Maggiolini. Civiche Raccolte Artistiche, Milan.

376 *(above right)* Card table, veneered and inlaid with varied woods. Italian (Lombardy), end of 18th century; by Giuseppe Maggiolini. Civiche Raccolte Artistiche, Milan (formerly in Palazzo Reale).

377 *(right)* Commode with marquetry of varied woods and ormolu mounts. Spanish, c. 1770. Although rather similar to Boulle marquetry, this is without doubt a Spanish work. Palacio Real, Madrid (by courtesy of Patrimonio Nacional, Madrid).

378 *(left)* Artist's work cabinet, with inlay of different woods and a central lacquer panel. Dutch, late 18th century. A small drawer at the side of this easel-like cabinet is meant to hold brushes, pencils, and other artist's materials. Rijksmuseum, Amsterdam.

379 *(below)* Dresser-commode with marquetry panels. Dutch, late 18th century. The top may be raised like a lid to uncover a water container and basin. Rijksmuseum, Amsterdam.

380　Bedroom furnished with Dutch neoclassic
furniture. Dutch, late 18th century. The bed,
which retains the original covering of its era,
follows the French Louis XVI style.
Rijksmuseum, Amsterdam.

381 (*below*) Dressing table and chair of steel, with copper and brass ornament. Russian, early 19th century. Metal furniture was a specialty of the workshops of Tula. Pavlovskij Palace Museum, Leningrad.

382 (*right*) Side table and pier glass of carved and silvered wood, inset with painted panels and medallions resembling Wedgwood ware. German, late 18th century. Schloss Charlottenburg, Berlin.

383 So-called "Chinese Room," in Schloss
Charlottenburg, Berlin. German, c. 1790;
decorated by a painter named Verona for
Frederick William II of Prussia. This interior
reflects a mixture of *chinoiserie* and neoclassic
style, with Chinese-motif *papiers peints* and
objets used in a formal neoclassic setting.

228

384 Jewel cabinet of mahogany, with fine ormolu mounts. French, late 18th century (Louis XVI period); made by Jean Henri Riesener for the Comtesse de Provence, whose coat of arms is displayed between the ormolu Cupids. The candelabra date from the early 19th century. (Reproduced by gracious permission of Her Majesty Queen Elizabeth II; copyright reserved)

Empire, Regency, and Federal

(Plates 384–445)

In this section we have sought to cover the two main approaches to classical taste which were active in the early years of the 19th century and which, for convenience, we term Empire and Regency, reflecting the two main political foci of the day. Napoleon, controlling almost the whole continent of Europe, imposed his taste upon it. England influenced the remainder, including the United States, which had its own Federal style and, later, a minor strain of Empire more or less concurrent with the European trends (pp. 260–263).

The differences between the two large tendencies of the day, as well as the stylistic exchanges here and there, are readily manifest in the two main groups of plates in this section (pp. 228, 233–247; and 254–259).

That all the elements of Empire were already latent in pieces made for the prerevolutionary court is clearly shown by a comparison of the first two examples (Plates 384–385). The whole of early-19th-century neoclassicism was a natural reaction against too much fuss and frippery. London reacted in the same way. In revolutionary France and under the Directorate, a certain modesty might be expected (e.g., pp. 234–235), but a return to privilege and luxury was not far off and even before Napoleon had reestablished his court, extremely elegant and decorative work was done for those who led society. Once Napoleon was established in power, there was no doubt left at all about where the influence lay, and everything that craftsmanship and money could provide was turned toward decorating the imperial background. Naturally, the Emperor's satellites elsewhere also conformed, and what they did can be seen in subsequent illustrations here (pp. 247–253).

If the use of "Empire" served to promote Napoleon's imperial dreams, Regency too was on occasion a political as well as an aesthetic gesture. It seems logical to presume that the adoptions and adaptations of the common stock of classical knowledge on either side of the Channel reflected the national character and politics. These certainly follow logically upon the characteristics that have been shown in previous sections.

In France, if the Revolution put a sudden stop to a trade which was essentially devoted to the gratification of the very people whose heads were being severed, the trade very quickly recovered and adjusted itself to public patronage and also, later, to more personal commissions from profiteers. The classicism that had catered to the court merely switched from agreeable dilettantism to a more serious reflection of what romantic idealists saw as the probity, patriotism, and sincerity of consular Rome. On saber-legged consular thrones in front of the most formal simple walls, republican politicians and their toadies, and romantic imitators across the frontiers could play at aping noble Romans and extol the wonders of democracy among a starving populace.

When finally the new empire came, it needed but a switch back to imperial Rome to find the proper mode of expression for its time. The same firms, such as the Jacob brothers, and just as often presumably the same craftsmen, moved from one good client to another, from royal to republican to imperial patronage and then back to Restauration. It mattered little as long as bills were paid. If the objects were but different interpretations of the ancients, one feature stands out: their quality remained superb.

The average Anglo-Saxon child is liable to leave

school with the history of the decades around 1800 delimited roughly thus: 1789, French Revolution; 1815, Battle of Waterloo. In between came something called the Battle of Trafalgar, won by an admiral named Nelson who asked his captain to kiss him as he lay dying on the deck of his flagship. If such a sentence seems inappropriate in a book on furniture, it may well prove justified if we give a few notes on the period between the dates, from the other side. Between these dates a new style developed, dominated nine-tenths of European taste, and then faded out. We call it "Empire," and though sometimes unfashionable as compared with Regency today, its relative importance would have reversed the scales in 1810.

Although the Revolution dates from 1789, the king was not executed till five years later, in 1794. People did not basically want tradition to be rooted out, and this was reflected in the furniture of those years. By 1795 the Republic had made peace wherever it could; but then, by 1796, news started to sound ominous— "Bonaparte defeats...." Following Bonaparte's ascendancy came the establishment of a number of republics. Lombardy, Holland, Switzerland, Naples, and Liguria, as they were then known, and others made themselves in some way independent in whole or part, and in being inspired to do so were biased in favor of the French. Then comes a further list of entries in the chronology such as "1804 – Napoleon made emperor; 1806 – Joseph Bonaparte created King of Naples; Eliza, Princess of . . . ; Pauline, Princess of . . . ; Murat . . . ; Berthier . . . ; Louis Bonaparte created King of Holland. 1807 – Jerome made King of Westphalia. 1808 – Joseph named King of Spain . . ." and on and on. Meanwhile the Confederation of the Rhine had transformed old Germany, and the Holy Roman emperor could marry his Catholic daughter to a divorced commoner. Within a fairly brief span, this was a change in the course of history on a scale that makes even Hitler's rise and conquests seem modest. Can we then wonder that the Empire style spread everywhere that this military genius ruled in person or by proxy. It also explains why, when Napoleon's day was over, the *gout anglais* fell heir to a vogue that arose in sympathy with or in gratitude for England's stand against all this hegemony.

Military genius apart, this revolution of Napoleon was also curious in that if it rose from barricades and fishwives' riots, it was quickly turned by his astuteness and guidance into a fairly peaceful takeover of existing privileged societies once the battle had been won. If he changed a dozen dynasties, or took over where they had left off, rule by the old style of monarchy and an aristocratic elite went on. New ministers might come, but they were not called "Citizen" or "Comrade," instead they quickly became dukes, princes, barons, and the like. Thus the whole ruling machine was kept in order as it had always been. The principles of Louis XIV remained, and at least with regard to furniture the courts and courtiers led the way, and did so in an ambiance in keeping with the dynasty then in control. Empire was the style that Napoleon supported, and so understandably Empire ousted all the Louis styles and the rococo, the baroque, and the lighter neoclassic that Marie-Antoinette had known. Such refurbishment was designed quite deliberately not only to promote the new but also to bury the past. This principle has not yet been abandoned.

What happened on the other side of the Channel was in logical sequence. There was inevitably some intellectual support for the revolutionaries of France at the outset, and if this was not of such a nature nor found among such people as would create a style of furniture, it did promote an atmosphere in which the severer trend to neoclassicism that was taking place on the Continent found an echo by the Thames. The clean lines and aggressive simplicity of the revolutionary interpretation of the style was also both practical and decorative and followed naturally as a reaction to the rather too pretty qualities in Adam, just as it had done in France by making a gesture against the affectations and preciosity of the court.

As with the Empire style in France, all the seeds of Regency had been planted by the last two decades of 18th-century neoclassicism. To some degree, the English Regency style stopped where the Directoire styles had stopped in Paris, with a strengthening and simplification of structure and a preference for consular Roman models rather than the imperial extravagances which were inevitably taken up by Napoleon, as a fit expression of the grandeur of his meteoric rise to the status of most powerful man on earth in his time.

English political opposition, as well as active war, generated strong influences against any further adoption of newer French style interpretations. In this case, use of the word "influences" is deliberate, for it is one of the interesting things about the time that whatever fears there may have been about "Boney" and whatever nationalistic waves might be encouraged by successive victories (especially Trafalgar), there remained quite a lot of contact with and not all that much hostility to the French per se. Indeed, many refugees from Napoleonic France and emigrés, among these the pretender to the throne himself, received the greatest kindness in their temporary home across the Channel. It was "John Bull" versus "Boney." If the French were "frogs," they always had been; and if one Englishman was cited as worth fifty of "them," he could afford to be tolerantly patronizing and perhaps even profit from time to time when they did something well. Very rich Englishmen might be criticized on occasion if they took advantage of the troubled times to acquire works of art and even furniture from royal sales in France, but they did it just the same—and not least among them England's monarch himself. In wealthier circles, also, there was as always a slight feeling of inferiority about matters of French taste, whether in clothes or furnishings. If some Englishmen went viciously "John Bullish," others paid at least a sneaking tribute to their French adversaries through the compliment of imitation.

For England, nonetheless, it would be a dangerous simplification to lay too great a stress on influences from abroad at this time, and it must be recalled that the neoclassic styles arose in the first place from a common international source, namely, the cultivated study of the ancients among rich and aristocratic dilettantes. If designs by Thomas Hope resemble drawings by people such as Percier, or vice versa, it was more likely due to common sources rather than to plagiarism by either, even though with the extension of publications most leading designers would undoubtedly be aware of each other's line. That is, the similarities reflected a general climate of taste of the period, and not necessarily the dominant influence of a few specific individuals.

What certainly did have effect all over Europe was the military side of the war. Fashions, whether in clothes or furnishings, took on a military air. The feminine domination that had been characteristic of the mid-18th century gave way to a man's world in the late 18th and early 19th centuries. Men's clothes were manly and designed to show to best advantage all the attributes of manly men, with wide shoulders and tight trousers; and those who were not actually on active service set out to look as handsome and forceful as they might have been in uniform. They drank and gambled in their clubs and homes, where

chairs and desks and other furnishings took on a strength and solidity that could support rough treatment and also serve as appropriate background for the new male image. All this looked well and suited to its purpose; military motifs enhanced much of the period's design, particularly in such decorative adjuncts as the spears and fasces of curtain rods, camp bed drapes, crossed-sword stools, and other such martial accessories.

Little wonder, then, that the excessive elegancies of the 18th century declined in this politico-cultural climate, and if some of the simpler and more conservative of 18th-century designs continued, furniture in general (unless designed especially for women) took on robuster qualities. Nevertheless, most of it retained a modicum of good design, since fashion was still an upper-class or elitist affair. Not until the second quarter of the 19th century, when bourgeois dominance set in, did clumsy, stolid weightiness and cosy plush take over in design.

In this persistence of selectivity, a factor that made no small contribution was the increasing practice of the leading architects to treat furniture as part and parcel of their whole design. This tendency was not entirely new. As we have seen, rococo artists did this very much, and Renaissance men before them. In England, Kent had played his part in this trend, but probably it was the all-embracing design practices of Adam that brought such integrated design on an even greater scale. The ideal he sought was that not a single moulding or doorknob should be incorporated in a room unless it emanated from his invention, and with the very richest of his clients he succeeded grandly. Now, with artists such as Henry Holland at Carlton House and Brighton and others, the versatile architect replaced the cabinetmaker/interior decorator who had emerged towards the middle of the 18th century. At the same time, for lesser commissions the retail shop was taking over more and more, catering to the vastly greater needs of and distribution for the rapidly growing consumer class. Though the mass production soon to come had not yet entirely altered the structure of the craft, old-time leaders like the great cabinetmakers of the 18th century were already dying out.

385 Jewel cabinet of figured mahogany, with
ormolu mounts and mother-of-pearl inlay.
French, 1809 (Empire period); made by Jacob
Desmalter for the Empress Josephine. The
design came chiefly from the sculptor Chaudet,
and the mounts were executed by Pierre
Philippe Thomire. Louvre, Paris.

233

386 *(left)* Mahogany side table, partly gilded and inlaid with ebony and pewter. French, 1796; by the Jacob brothers. Grand Trianon, Versailles.

387 *(below)* Mahogany bed, with ormolu mounts and carved bronze-finish figures of swans at the corners. French, early 19th century. Musée des Arts Décoratifs, Paris.

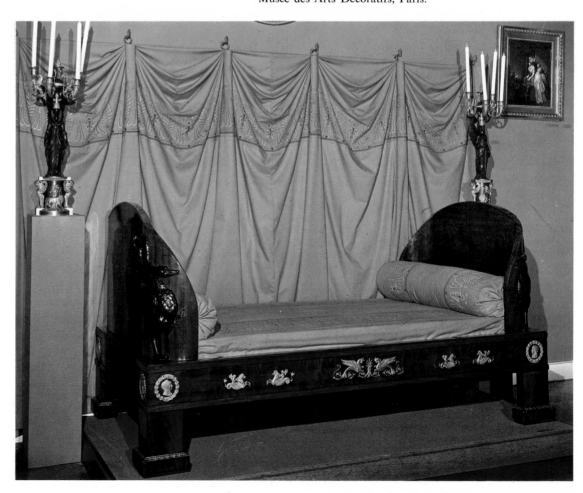

388 Music room at the Château de Malmaison,
near Paris. French, decorated and furnished
c. 1800. The decorations are by Charles Percier
and Pierre F. L. Fontaine; the furniture was
made by the Jacob brothers of partly gilded
mahogany and ebonized wood. The mahogany
pianoforte is credited to the Erard brothers
(1812).

389 *(above)* Armchair of carved wood, painted and gilded. Russian, early 19th century; based on design by A. N. Voronichin. Note particularly the gilt armrests in the form of eagles' wings. Pavlovskij Palace Museum, Leningrad.

390 *(right)* Tripod stand (*Athénienne*) of gilded and bronze-finished wood. French, early 19th century (Empire). Private collection.

392 *(above)* Stool of carved and gilded wood.
French, probably c. 1805; by Jacob Desmalter.
The form is of the traditional folding type,
but the legs are carved in the shape of
crossed swords. Victoria and Albert Museum,
London (from Château de Saint-Cloud).

391 *(above)* Armchair of carved wood, painted
and gilded. French, early 19th century
(Directoire period). Musée des Arts Décoratifs,
Paris.

393 *(right)* Carved stool, painted and gilded.
Italian (Naples), c. 1810. Made for the court of
Murat, this is similar to one made by Georges
Jacob for Saint-Cloud. Palazzo Reale, Naples.

237

394 *(left)* Table with top and base of thuya wood, with partly gilded bronze supports. French, early 19th century. Victoria and Albert Museum, London (from the apartments of Napoleon III at Saint-Cloud).

395 *(below)* Needlework frame of mahogany, with ormolu mounts. French, c. 1811; by Alexandre Maigret. The mahogany chair is of the type made by the Jacob brothers in the Directoire period. Château de Fontainebleau.

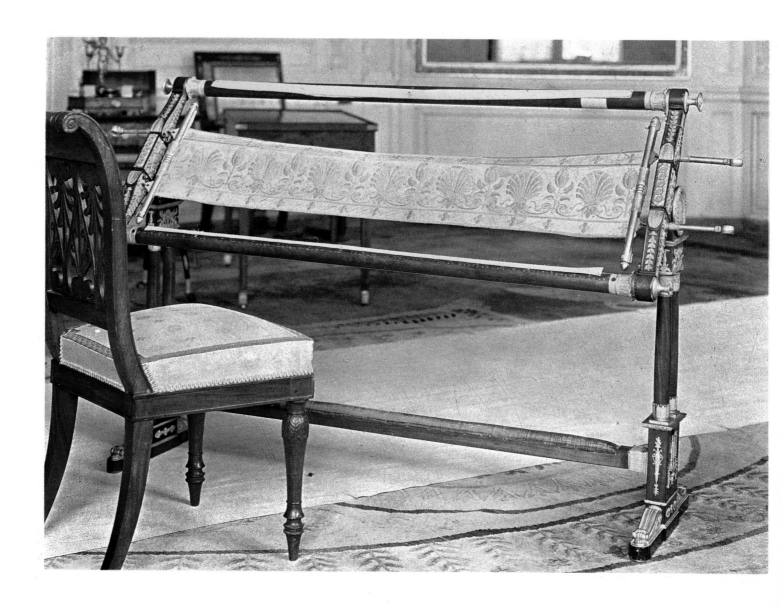

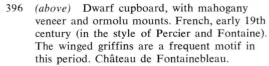

396 *(above)* Dwarf cupboard, with mahogany veneer and ormolu mounts. French, early 19th century (in the style of Percier and Fontaine). The winged griffins are a frequent motif in this period. Château de Fontainebleau.

397 *(left)* Secrétaire of figured mahogany, with ormolu mounts and figural appliqués. French, c. 1810; part of a suite made for Murat, probably by Adam Weisweiler. The central panel contains an allegory of Love and Wisdom. Palazzo Reale, Naples.

398 *(above)* Mahogany cheval mirror, or dressing glass (*Psyché*), with ormolu mounts, candle brackets, and supports. French, early 19th century; based on a design by Charles Percier and made by Jacob Desmalter. Winged chimera supports are another favored motif of this period. Musée National du Château de Compiègne.

399 *(above right)* Mahogany writing desk. French, c. 1800; designed by Charles Percier and executed by the Jacob brothers. This piece was ordered by Madame Napoléon Bonaparte for the Bonapartes' private house in Paris. Grand Trianon, Versailles.

400 *(right)* Center table of mahogany, inlaid with ebony and pewter. French, c. 1806; given by Napoleon to the Crown Prince of Bavaria. The Egyptian head supports are of bronze, the top surface of porcelain, and the frieze is set with biscuit Sèvres in imitation of Wedgwood ware. The painted porcelain top by Georg Lamprecht depicts "The Lion Calling the Other Animals" (1786). Bayerisches Nationalmuseum, Munich.

240

401 Marble-topped double console of ash,
supported by four ormolu caryatids. French,
early 19th century; by Jacob Desmalter.
Grand Trianon, Versailles.

402 (left) Bedroom of Empress Josephine in the Château de Malmaison, near Paris. French, early 19th century. The gilded bed was made by Jacob Desmalter about 1810; the worktable with mirror, of the same period, is by M. G. Biennais.

403 (below) "Gondola" armchairs, decorated with carved, painted and gilded swans. French, early 19th century (Empire period); made by Jacob Desmalter, after a design by Charles Percier, for the imperial chambers at Saint-Cloud. Château de Malmaison, near Paris.

404 (right) Formal bedchamber-reception room, with Napoleon's bed from the Tuileries Palace. French, early 19th century (with alterations made for Louis-Philippe in 1837). The two bedside tables in Empire style (though dated 1837) are by Alphonse Jacob. Grand Trianon, Versailles.

405 *(above)*   Mahogany bed with ormolu mounts
(*lit en bateau* or *à la turque*). French, early 19th
century. Musée des Arts Décoratifs, Paris.

406 *(right)*   Secrétaire with burr-elm veneer and
ormolu mounts. French, early 19th century;
made by J. J. Werner for Hôtel des Invalides.
Musée des Arts Décoratifs, Paris.

407 (above) Cradle of amboyna, with ormolu ornament. French, 1811; made by Jacob Desmalter for the King of Rome (the son of Napoleon). The metalwork is by Pierre Philippe Thomire, after designs by Prud'hon; during the Restoration years, the original ormolu eagle supporting the curtain ring was replaced by the allegorical figure of Fame. Louvre, Paris.

408 (right) Mahogany "gondola" chair, with carved and gilded dolphin motif. French, early 19th century; by Jacob Desmalter. Musée des Arts Décoratifs, Paris.

409 Furniture of carved and gilded wood, covered with Lyons cut velvet, made for Napoleon's private apartments at Fontainebleau. French, c. 1810; by P. G. Brion. Included here is a so-called *paumier* sofa. Château de Fontainebleau.

410 *(far left)* Armchair of carved and painted wood. French, early 19th century. The covering is 18th-century Beauvais tapestry. Château de Fontainebleau.

411 *(left)* Dressing table carved from white statuary marble. Italian (Naples), c. 1825 (late Empire period). Reggia, Caserta.

412 *(right)* So-called "Platinum Room," in the Casita del Labrador, Aranjuez. French, early 19th century; designed by Charles Percier and Pierre F. L. Fontaine and made in Paris. The mahogany paneling is inlaid with platinum. The panels have paintings of the Seasons by Girodet and views by Bidault and Thibault (by courtesy of Patrimonio Nacional, Madrid).

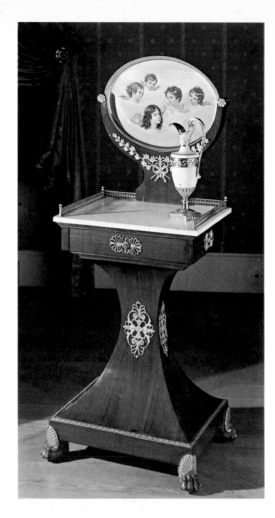

413 *(right)* Side table of painted wood, with fine metal mounts and a porcelain top painted in Pompeian style. Austrian, early 19th century. Bundessammlung Alter Stilmöbel, Vienna.

414 *(far right)* Small dressing table of purplewood, with metal mounts. German, c. 1815. The oval frame now containing painted porcelain was originally a mirror. Residenzmuseum, Munich.

415 *(below)* Mahogany commode, with amboyna panels inset with classical panels and medallions in engraved mirror glass. Spanish, late 18th century. Palacio Real, Madrid (by courtesy of Patrimonio Nacional, Madrid).

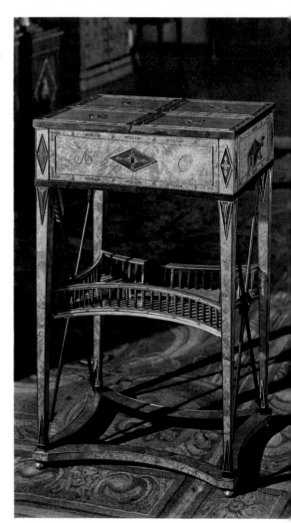

416 *(right)* Worktable, with Hungarian ash veneer and silvered metal mounts. Austrian (Vienna), c. 1810. Österreichisches Museum für Angewandte Kunst, Vienna.

417 Writing table, inlaid with varied woods and mounted with ormolu relief plaques showing scenes of Spanish history. Spanish, early 19th century. Escorial Palace (by courtesy of Patrimonio Nacional, Madrid).

418 *(above)* Bronze stool, partly gilded, with crossed supports in Egyptian style. Spanish, early 19th century. Casita del Labrador, Aranjuez (by courtesy of Patrimonio Nacional, Madrid).

419 *(right)* Mahogany armchair, with gilded carving and swan heads. Spanish, early 19th century. Palace of La Granja (by courtesy of Patrimonio Nacional, Madrid).

420 *(left)* Mahogany officer's chair, with "gondola" back, designed so that the occupant could sit without removing his sword. French, c. 1795 (Directoire period); in the style of Georges Jacob. Musée des Arts Décoratifs, Paris.

421 *(below)* Cherrywood sofa *(méridienne* type), with original covering. Italian (Tuscany), early 19th century. Collection of Doctor Virgilio Gaddi, Florence.

422 *(below left)* Small cabinet in form of a drum, made of various woods, carved and gilded. Italian, 1807; from a set of furniture made by Giovanni Socci of Florence for Princess Elisa Baciocchi, sister of Napoleon. Museo Napoleonico, Rome.

251

423 *(left)* Long-case clock of mahogany, surmounted by the Prussian eagle. German, early 19th century (Empire period). The clockworks are signed by D. Nevir. Schloss Charlottenburg, Berlin.

424 *(below)* Mahogany dressing table. Austrian (Vienna), early 19th century. The distinctive oval contour and sideward-opening drawers make this restrained *toilette* interesting. Bundessammlung Alter Stilmöbel, Vienna.

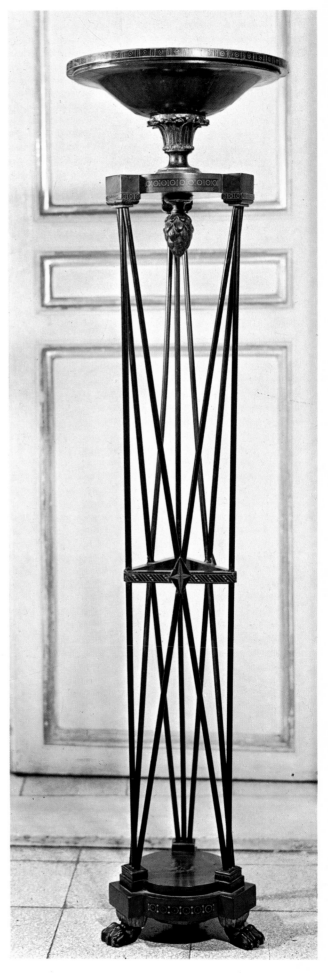

426 *(below)* Candlestand (*torchère* or *guéridon*) of mahogany and bronze. German, early 19th century. The linear triangular form is derived from ancient examples recovered at Pompeii. Collection of Mario Praz, Rome.

425 *(above)* Secrétaire (detail), with case mainly of mahogany and architectural interior details of varied materials. Austrian (Vienna), dated 1813; signed by Johann Haertl. Österreichisches Museum für Angewandte Kunst, Vienna.

427 *(right)* Mahogany tripod stand, with lion monopodia. English, c. 1810; made for the Duke of Newcastle. The design is after one published by Thomas Hope (*Household Furniture and Interior Decoration*, 1807). Victoria and Albert Museum, London.

428 *(below)* Sofa of gilded wood, carved with animal heads and lion monopodia supports. English, 1805; made by the manufactory Gillow for Kimmel Park. Victoria and Albert Museum, London.

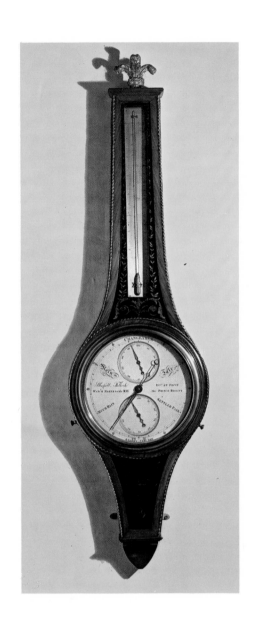

429 (above) Rosewood sideboard, with fine brass mounts and molding. English, c. 1820. Victoria and Albert Museum, London.

430 (right) Mahogany barometer, with painted glass panels and gilt-brass ornament. English, c. 1800. The dial is signed by J. Russell, clockmaker to the Prince of Wales. Victoria and Albert Museum, London.

431 Mahogany dressing table, with carved hoofed feet. English; based on a design from George Smith's *Collection of Designs for Household Furniture* (1808). Victoria and Albert Museum, London.

432 Regency interior. English, c. 1810–15. The mahogany library table is carved with Egyptian motifs. The painted wooden chair behind the desk was inspired by a design of Thomas Hope (1807). Victoria and Albert Museum, London.

433 *(left)* Mahogany table, with inlay of ebony and silver. English, early 19th century; designed by Thomas Hope for his own residence and published in his *Household Furniture and Interior Decoration* (1807). Victoria and Albert Museum, London.

434 *(below left)* Armchair of carved wood, ebonized and gilded, in the "Egyptian" taste. English, 1806; similar to a design by George Smith of 1804, included in his *Collection of Designs for Household Furniture* (1808). Victoria and Albert Museum, London.

435 *(below)* Mahogany X-shaped chair (curule type), with backrest carved in a design taken from a Roman sarcophagus. English, early 19th century; based on a published design by Thomas Hope (1807). Private collection, England.

436 *(above)* Daybed, or "Grecian couch," of carved and gilded wood. English, early 19th century (Regency period); taken from an illustration in Sheraton's *Encyclopaedia* (1805). Private collection, England.

437 *(right)* Carved mahogany armchair. English, c. 1820. Victoria and Albert Museum, London.

438 *(below)* Bureau-bookcase, veneered with zebra wood. English, probably 1808 (datable by the watercolors behind the glass panes, signed J. Baynes). Victoria and Albert Museum, London.

439 *(right)* Mahogany bookcase, with bronze mounts and painted stucco busts. English, c. 1808; derived from a design in Sheraton's *Encyclopaedia*. Victoria and Albert Museum, London.

440 Imlay Room. American, c. 1805. The chairs and tables of painted wood were very likely made in Baltimore. Henry Francis du Pont Winterthur Museum, Wilmington, Delaware.

441 *(left)* Franklin Room. American, end of 18th century. Except for the center table and sofa, which are by New York craftsmen, this room is furnished with Massachusetts-made pieces. Henry Francis du Pont Winterthur Museum, Wilmington, Delaware.

442 *(below)* Mahogany desk, with folding writing surface and enameled drawer pulls. American (Boston), c. 1800; bears the mark "John Seymour & Son," who were active in Boston in the decade 1794–1804. Henry Francis du Pont Winterthur Museum, Wilmington, Delaware.

443 *(left)* Phyfe Room. American, c. 1805. The side chairs, from a New York house, are by the celebrated American cabinetmaker Duncan Phyfe. The elaborate gilt mantel mirror is from Albany. Henry Francis du Pont Winterthur Museum, Wilmington, Delaware.

261

444 *(above)* McIntire Bedroom. American, furnished with items dating from the Federal period. Although named in honor of Samuel McIntire, a leading late-18th-century American cabinetmaker, who built several of the chairs seen here, this room is a veritable treasury of early American craftsmanship. The woodwork is from the Philadelphia townhouse built by Robert Wellford in 1812. The marble-topped bedtable is attributed to John Seymour; the bed (1796) is by Jacob Wayne of Philadelphia, and the satinwood sewing table by Ephraim Haines, also of Philadelphia. Henry Francis du Pont Winterthur Museum, Wilmington, Delaware.

445 *(right)* Empire Parlor. American, furnished with items in Empire style (c. 1815–40). The woodwork is from a house built in Albany by General Rufus King in 1839. The Italian marble mantel is from a New York City townhouse. The side table next to the fireplace expresses the basic architectural form of Empire furniture. The stencil-decorated worktable in the background (1834–36) is by Roswell A. Hubbard; the pillar-base table in the center has a top painted by Lewis Brantz. The various porcelains, some with patriotic motifs, are both French and American. Henry Francis du Pont Winterthur Museum, Wilmington, Delaware.

446 Salon des Glaces of the Grand Trianon, Versailles. French, mostly 1805–10. The armchairs, console, and mahogany tables are by Jacob Desmalter; the pianoforte is by Erard. The rare pendulum clock in the foreground, designed as a bouquet of flowers, is signed "Lepine et Neveu" and dates from 1826. The paneling of the room is of the Louis XIV period.

The Mid-19th Century

(Plates 446–507)

Although there was some stiff or sycophantic reaction against Napoleon after 1815, and in some areas a tendency for design to follow politics and turn to more English ways, by no means the whole of Europe swung away from the Empire taste. In some areas, in the early decades of the 19th century, furniture lost something of the ormolu and the very imperial grandeur. The basic forms were rounded off to become a little less severe, but their neoclassic ancestry remains manifest. The process is clearly seen in the difference between the plates in the previous section and the first of these (Plate 446). A movement like Biedermeier emphasizes that, for the Continent as a whole, it was the French models rather than the simpler English Regency which held sway. Nevertheless, this last court style was destined to be superseded by a new-rich bourgeois taste, greedily ready to adopt or adapt (often rather badly) any pattern that had gone before. Thus, we find a stream of such interpretations at this time, from Gothic to a grand muddle in which anything from papier mâché to adapted Sheraton, Spanish, or Charles II might have had a hand. China, India, the Renaissance, Chippendale, and even Sir Walter Scott all made their contributions to the eclectic trend. All the Louis styles—along with a somewhat unreceptive imagination—also appeared, sometimes mingled in a single piece, and so the sorry story of pastiche progresses. Anything from Versailles or St. Peter's, or from maharajas to Medicis, was pillaged to give the weight of confidence, respectability, and a background of importance to a vast new-rich society in a different world. Three parts ashamed of their lack of pedigree, whatever pride and truculence they might draw from their wealth, they required some ancestral precedent. It was a pretty crude world in many ways, made the more so because those who in earlier periods had maintained the old tradition of aristocratic dignity and elite apartness also turned toward the fleshpots. The final accolade for all this from royal sources is shown in some truly magnificent examples (Plates 505, 507). These fabrications, on which all the rest and baroque too were flung in a profusion of gold and precious materials and elaborate carving, are almost splendid in their shameless flaunting of wealth and luxury. For the first time, both patrons and craftsmen delighted openly in showy and plushy comfort. In this at least, they represent the ideal of their time.

If the Field of the Cloth of Gold had served as a splendid set piece in the Middle Ages, so the "Great Exhibitions" of the 19th century—and, in particular, that of 1851 in England—served a similar purpose for the fireworks of mid-19th-century mercantile advance. Never in the history of the world had there been such a display of "arts and manufactures" that an astonished bourgeoisie might congratulate itself on its achievements and industry. In this, we must make no mistake; it was the triumph of the middle classes that these exhibitions stressed. It was they who had risked their money, proved their capacity to organize, and shown what thrift and commercial acumen might achieve. What now lay before the world to admire was no result of quarterings passed down from medieval times, even if most areas still retained a monarchy of sorts and continued to pay homage to noble titles. While the contribution of the artisans and craftsmen was pompously acknowledged in blurbs and catalogues, in the new scheme of things their efforts meant little more than the contribution of the cow to milk—now so earnestly enjoined for little boys and girls whose parents could afford it. It was the middle classes who made the whole thing work. From the Danube to the Eastern seaboard of America, portly and portentous "gentlemen" (as they were fast becoming even though in "trade") stepped bravely out to church accompanied by wives and families to worship God and show their neighbors that they were virtually His representatives on earth, or they looked out from the windows of their pseudo castles or knobbed pretentious villas—generally placed close to the factory they owned. It was to the declaration of this principle and to this achievement that the ambitious exhibition trappings were dedicated. Gone was all the elegance of 18th-century courts and aristocrat-inspired design, and in its place came a vast encumbering display of solid, tangible, and very worldly worth. As noted in other times of bourgeois lead in civic arts and building, such a feature had always emerged.

Though it would be silly to pretend that many a rising banker or successful retired tradesman did not seek a title, or at least attempt to buy a manor in the hope that his heirs might rank as gentry or noblemen, at the same time many a duke or baron was prepared to modify his old ideals and seek the comforts and advantages these new developments were bringing. As a result, many an ancient castle or even charming, comparatively recent 18th-century houses were pulled down to be replaced by medieval battlements and crockets in the best romantic, Wagnerian, Walter Scott compromise that the manufacturers commissioned to feel themselves like dukes of ancient lineage. If Ludwig of Bavaria could feel constrained to raise a palace like a nouveau financier's dream, little wonder that much lower down the scale shopkeepers and factory managers had designed for themselves "important" houses in their villages, to set them up before their fellows. There is scarcely a village in Europe that did not have some such strange abortion of design put up by a local worthy for his lasting fame. An even if the mayor had spared his own kith and kin from such inheritance, he probably encouraged such a public building for the honor and greater glory of his town. Soon stores and hostelries began to follow suit, lest they be relegated to the past. Railways too were prodigal in this respect. No wonder that the great exhibitions prospered and that the items they displayed had to be mass-produced to meet growing demand everywhere. As solid weight of solid and expensive wood paraded costliness and solid worth for all to see, the finest furniture of the time was

made of these. As carving and intricacy bespoke of time and money to create them, so lavish carving and intricacy were sought as luxury adjuncts to the furniture. Gone were the days when the rising bourgeois tried to ape the upper classes by over-refinement and gentility, such as was evident in Sheraton and early Empire pieces. Now the affluent bourgeois gloried in his own surroundings and station and, though perhaps unwittingly, in vulgarity. This lay at the root of the mid-19th-century jungle of design for the upper classes that followed.

Yet it had taken time for all this to evolve, and though the beginnings of this international industrialist group of styles were developing in the 1830s, and were even latent in the 1820s, the old political factors of the first part of the century still made their impact on basic styles. The key to these was perhaps still Napoleon. Even dead, and even if his influence was no longer all-dominating as it had been at the height of his career, its effects were still strong in countries that had a Napoleonic dynasty or pretenders. These, we must remember, included not only such direct lines as in France, Spain, or Naples or the Bernadottes in the north, but also several German territories whose rise and even existence as kingdoms owed so much to the French emperor's design and might. Bavaria and Württemberg, for example, had good reason to be drawn into that camp Even Austria was not at all ashamed of marriage ties when political advantage seemed to be involved. The banishments and "restorations," whether of Bourbon or Napoleonic candidates, made themselves felt widely outside France as well and were reflected in furniture by waves of Empire, or otherwise as designers revived the earlier modes of whatever dynasty was currently in power. In reaction, moreover, there might even be a revival of "English" taste in areas which had always regarded Napoleon as an aggressor rather than as a hero of their country.

Fortunately, in most places these changes took place reasonably quietly, and the governments went about their business and ordinary citizens continued to build up wealth and further industry. As transport improved, which it did with great rapidity once the railways had come in, more people left the countryside and rural livelihoods to go to the towns surrounding the factories and mills and mines. Here the ever-growing wealth of vast new urban and suburban middle-class societies created an unparalleled demand for furniture, so that mass production of furnishings soon developed. The great stream of products served as background for the status seekers of this middle-class society, imbued with hierarchies as distinct as ever. They also set the tone for a new attitude to self and to the world which these people embraced.

Inside the villas of suburbia and newer houses everywhere, a maze of styles characterized the rooms, almost all reflecting some earlier design. To join the hangovers from Empire or the English taste, the Regency and Biedermeier, the 1830s, 1840s, and 1850s brought in anything from Walter Scott Gothic—the novelist was quite as popular abroad as at home in England—to a spate of very literary "Dumas Renaissance," especially in France. Pastiches of "tous les Louis" filled salons and parlors around the world, and even had great vogue with maharajas. Assertive, misshapen, misinterpreted baroque had no

little following in an affluent industrialized world which no longer thought itself inferior but which gloried in its presentation and surroundings.

So often spoken of as "Victorian" by the English-speaking world, this was nevertheless an international, even interclass (if rich enough) phenomenon. If the English queen, with her small-town German ways dominating all her great estate, has since become the symbol of the times, it may not be inapposite. Even if she was the "First Lady" of her land—or possibly, of the world at that time—it did not stop her from being typical of millions of her subjects or those of other monarchs or authorities elsewhere in this period. The people were not "Victorian" because they aped their queen; rather, the name survived because she was the archetype of the Zeitgeist of her day.

447 *(right)* Watercolor of a Neapolitan interior. Italian, first half of 19th century. Collection of Desmond Fitzgerald, London.

448 *(below)* Early-19th-century French furniture: dressing table of solid ash by A. T. Baudouin (1809); maple commode by J. J. Werner (1819); chairs by P. Marcion (c. 1810); the round table and looking glass (*Psyché*) are of slightly later date. Grand Trianon, Versailles.

449 *(right)* Marble-topped mahogany writing desk, inscribed in Italian "To Her Majesty Maria Teresa Isabella, Queen of the Two Sicilies, in homage from Giuseppe P.pe Manganelli." Italian, early 19th century. The elliptical form and the inward-facing caryatid supports make this an unusual piece. Inlaid in the marble top are three granite medallions with classical motifs. Palazzo Reale, Naples.

450 *(below)* Table of carved, painted and gilded wood. Italian (Naples), 1825–30. The top is decorated with a watercolor under glass. Reggia di Capodimonte, Naples.

451 *(right)* Mahogany table with ormolu mounts. Italian, early 19th century. In this multipurpose piece, the stretchers hold a fishbowl; the upper part is designed as a planter, with a place for a birdcage surmounted by an ormolu figure of Fortune. Reggia di Capodimonte, Naples.

452 *(below)* Sofa of dark wood. Russian, early 19th century; designed by A. N. Voronichin. This piece, from the bedroom of Czarina Maria Feodorovna, reflects a Russian adaptation of the French Empire style. Pavlovskij Palace Museum, Leningrad.

453 *(left)* Armchair of *bois clair*, inlaid with palisander. French, probably second quarter of 19th century; by G. Alphonse Jacob, last of this famed family of *ébénistes*. Musée des Arts Décoratifs, Paris.

454 *(above)* Secrétaire-commode of figured maple, with amaranth inlay. French, c. 1825. The top drawer front pulls out to become a writing surface with delicate baluster sides. Galerie Nicole Gérard, Paris.

455 *(right)* Secrétaire of ash, with mirror glass and ormolu mounts. French, c. 1825 (Restoration period); bears the mark of J. J. Werner. The maple chair with Gothic backrest dates from about 1830. Musée des Arts Décoratifs, Paris.

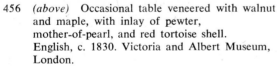

456 *(above)* Occasional table veneered with walnut
and maple, with inlay of pewter,
mother-of-pearl, and red tortoise shell.
English, c. 1830. Victoria and Albert Museum,
London.

457 *(above right)* Writing desk veneered with
cherrywood. Italian, early 19th century; from
the Villa Mansi at Segromigno (Lucca).
The bronze lock bears the coat of arms of the
Mansi family; the lion monopodia are of
carved, painted and gilded wood.
Private collection.

458 *(right)* Cylinder bureau of figured ash, inlaid
with amaranth. French, c. 1825; made by
L. F. Puteaux. Musée Carnavalet, Paris.

459 Billiard table of maple and ebony. French,
c. 1820. Light-colored woods such as maple
enjoyed particular favor in the time of
Louis XVIII and Charles X. Castaing Collection,
Paris.

460 *(above)* Bed made of ash and burr elm, with rosewood inlay. French, exhibited at the Paris Exposition of 1827 by its maker, François Baudry. The bedside table is of ash, with amaranth inlay and ormolu mounts. Musée des Arts Décoratifs, Paris.

461 *(right)* Maple chair with ormolu mounts. French, c. 1820. The backrest is carved in a simulated drapery design for decorative effect. Musée des Arts Décoratifs, Paris.

462 *(above)* Mahogany cradle, with gilt-brass mounts. French, first quarter of 19th century. Collection of Mario Praz, Rome.

463 *(right)* Maple "gondola" chair, with rosewood inlay. French, c. 1820. Musée des Arts Décoratifs, Paris.

464 *(above)* Mahogany armchair, with ormolu mounts and its original needlework cover. French, early 19th century; by P. A. Bellange. Collection of Mario Praz, Rome.

465 *(above right)* Circular table of pale mahogany. French, dated 1837; by Jacob Desmalter. The frieze band around the edge contains eight curved-front drawers. Grand Trianon, Versailles.

466 *(right)* Chair veneered with mahogany. Probably Russian (or by a Russian craftsman working in Western Europe), c. 1830. Galleria U. Dal Guerra, Florence.

467 *(right)* Mahogany dressing table. Spanish, second quarter of 19th century. This eclectic combination of neoclassic motifs was undoubtedly inspired by French Empire style. Palacio de Aranjuez (by courtesy of Patrimonio Nacional, Madrid).

468 *(below)* Mahogany writing desk. Swedish, c. 1830; by Adolph Friederik Ranft. This piece gives evidence of contact with the German Biedermeier taste. Nordiska Museet, Stockholm.

279

470 *(above)* Armchair of cherrywood, with backrest formed of colonnettes. Austrian (Vienna), early 19th century. Private collection.

469 *(above)* Mahogany secrétaire. Austrian (Vienna), early 19th century. The base and the lyre-shaped riser contain drawers and a fall-front writing table. Bayerisches Nationalmuseum, Munich.

471 *(right)* Sofa, with base veneered in ash. Austrian (Vienna), first half of 19th century. In this divan, styled more for comfort than for elegance, the legs seem to be folding under the weight of the generous padding. Bundessammlung Alter Stilmöbel, Vienna.

472 *(above)* Writing table of cherrywood.
Austrian (Vienna), c. 1820. The oval writing
surface and contoured drawers are supported
by tubular columns, the hollow tops of which
can be adapted as plant stands.
Österreichisches Museum für Angewandte
Kunst, Vienna.

473 *(right)* Mahogany roulette table, with pale
wood inlay and a revolving top. German, early
19th century. Schloss Pfaueninsel, near Berlin.

474 *(left)* Gothic Revival room in the Dairy of Schloss Pfaueninsel, near Berlin. German, early 19th century. The decoration was carried out by the stucco artist Constantin Sartori and the painter Verona.

475 *(right above)* Cast-iron seating furniture, originally designed for garden use. French, c. 1840. Musée des Arts Décoratifs, Paris.

476 *(right)* Neogothic console and armchairs of painted and gilded wood. Spanish, mid-19th century. Escorial Palace (by courtesy of Patrimonio Nacional, Madrid).

477 *(left)* Neogothic walnut writing table. English, c. 1855; based on a drawing by Augustus W. Pugin. Private collection, London.

478 *(below)* Neogothic walnut octagonal table. English, 1847; based on a drawing by Augustus W. Pugin, and perhaps executed by Crace & Sons. The splendor of Gothic tracery is here revived in the shape and lavish carving of the base. Victoria and Albert Museum, London.

479 *(right)* Mahogany armchair and walnut table. English, second quarter of 19th century, but table probably slightly earlier. The chair, from Eaton Hall in Cheshire, was perhaps designed by William Porden; the table, perhaps by Lewis Cottingham. Victoria and Albert Museum, London.

480 *(below)* Baldachin bed of *papier mâché*, with painted floral decoration and gilt-brass mounts. English (probably from Birmingham), c. 1850. Victoria and Albert Museum, London (donated by Queen Mary).

481 *(right)* Liqueur cabinet of *papier mâché*, with painted and gilt floral decoration. English, c. 1860. Inside is a metal tree rack to hold bottles and glasses. Victoria and Albert Museum, London.

482 *(left)* Dining and side chairs of painted *papier mâché*. English, mid-19th century. Victoria and Albert Museum, London.

483 *(below)* Settee, table, and Canterbury music rack of painted *papier mâché*. English, mid-19th century. Besides the painted floral motifs, there is also decorative mother-of-pearl inlay. Victoria and Albert Museum, London.

484 (left) Armchair of carved, painted and gilded
wood. Portuguese, early 19th century. The
decoration includes tiny delicately painted
panels of bucolic scenes. Museu Nacional de
Arte Antiga, Lisbon (by courtesy of Ministério
de Educaçao Nacional, Direcçao-Geral do
Eusino Superior e das Belas Artes).

485 (below) Sofa of carved, painted and gilded
wood. Spanish, c. 1800. The elaborately
carved, traceried backrests are characteristic of
Spanish furniture in this era. Palacio de
Aranjuez (by courtesy of Patrimonio Nacional,
Madrid).

486 (*above*) Table inlaid with different tinted
woods and straw. Italian (Sorrento), c. 1830;
signed Antonino Damorra. The table has a
12-sided top with a scalloped, inward-curving
edge. Museo Correale, Sorrento.

487 (*right*) Padded "conversation" chair, with
fringe border. French, mid-19th century
(Napoleon III period). Musée des Arts
Décoratifs, Paris.

488 (left) Miniature fireside chair (chauffeuse) of ebony. French, c. 1860 (Napoleon III period). Musée des Arts Décoratifs, Paris.

489 (below) Bed of carved and gilded wood. French, second half of 19th century (Second Empire). The mattress fits into a giant carved seashell, supported by gilt sirens and dolphins riding the waves below. Collection of Francis Stonor, London.

490 *(above)* Upholstered chairs, with frames veneered in kingwood, decorated with gilt-metal mouldings and painted porcelain plaques. French, mid-19th century. Private collection.

491–492 *(right)* Walnut chairs adorned with painted porcelain plaques. English, made for the Great Exhibition of 1851 by Henry Eyles of Bath. The Worcester porcelain plaques portray Queen Victoria and her consort Albert. Victoria and Albert Museum, London.

493 *(above)* Sofa of carved mahogany. English, c. 1835–40. In this sofa of high quality from the very beginning of the Victorian era, one still sees traces of Regency motifs in the richly carved details. Ipswich Museum and Art Galleries.

494 *(below)* Carved walnut table, inlaid with a porcelain plaque bearing the insignia of Brunswick. English, mid-19th century; carved by Henry Eyles of Bath. The intricate base is an indisputably virtuoso piece of carving. Victoria and Albert Museum, London.

495 *(left)* Console and mirror of gilded wood, comprising part of the furnishings of a room executed for Emilia Peruzzi. Italian (Florence), c. 1860 (Risorgimento era). The carving and gilding here have distinct echoes of the Tuscan baroque style. Palazzo Peruzzi, Florence.

496 *(below)* Table top with intarsia of varied woods and ivory. Italian, dated 1844. The intarsia scenes depict various holdings of the Massimo family. Palazzo Massimo, Rome.

497 *(below)* Ebony cabinet. English, shown at the Paris Exposition of 1855; made by the firm of Holland & Sons, after a design by the German architect Gottfried Semper. The Wedgwood porcelain plaque, done by George Gray, is after a painting by Mulready. Victoria and Albert Museum, London.

498 *(above)* Carved walnut armchair. French, c. 1860; by Guillaume Grohé, after a design by Ruprich-Robert. Château de Fontainebleau.

499 *(left)* Chair of pearwood, painted black. Possibly Swedish (in the French taste), c. 1870. Corresponding to the style of the Napoleon III period in France, this chair has elements of a not wholly successful revival of Louis XVI style. Nordiska Museet, Stockholm.

500 *(right)* Jardinière of carved, gilded wood. Italian (Naples), mid-19th century. This piece is a somewhat curious hybrid of baroque and Empire forms. Palazzo Reale, Naples.

501 *(below)* Table of carved, gilded wood, with marble top inlaid in *pietre dure*. Russian (St. Petersburg), c. 1850. Pavlovskij Palace Museum. Leningrad.

295

502 Ebony cabinet (*bas d'armoire*), inlaid with Italian *pietre dure* panels of the 17th century and ormolu mounts. French, c. 1835; made for Marshal Gérard. Musée des Arts Décoratifs, Paris.

503 *(left)* Writing desk, with palisander and rosewood veneer. Russian (in the French taste), c. 1860. This rococo pastiche, adorned with porcelain plaques and ormolu mounts, is a work in Napoleon III taste but of Russian provenance. Pavlovskij Palace Museum, Leningrad.

504 *(below)* Cabinet of inlaid walnut. French, c. 1850. Atop this low armoire is a bronze lion by Antoine Louis Barye. Musée des Arts Décoratifs, Paris.

505 Chair and writing table overlaid with malachite. Russian, mid-19th century. These sumptuous pieces were presented to Queen Isabella II of Spain by Czar Alexander II of Russia. Casita del Labrador, Aranjuez (by courtesy of Patrimonio Nacional, Madrid).

506 *(left)* Cabinet and mirror of carved, gilded wood, with bronze mounts and inset porcelain plaques. English, mid-19th century; designed by Eugène Prignot and executed by the firm of Jackson & Graham for the Paris Exposition of 1855. Victoria and Albert Museum, London.

507 *(below)* Bedroom of Queen Isabella II of Spain. Spanish, mid-19th century. Noteworthy here is the lavish use of gilt mounts on nearly all the furnishings, in addition to generous use of inlays. Palacio de Aranjuez (by courtesy of Patrimonio Nacional, Madrid).

508 *(right)* Washstand of painted and gilded wood. English, dated 1860; signed by the architect William Burges. Victoria and Albert Museum, London.

509 *(below)* Cabinet, veneered and inlaid with varied woods. English, dated 1862; designed by J. P. Seddon. The panels, painted with scenes from the honeymoon of René of Anjou, are by Ford Madox Brown, Edward Burne-Jones, William Morris, and Dante Gabriel Rossetti. Victoria and Albert Museum, London.

The Artist-Craftsman

(Plates 508—544)

This last section touches on a manifestation which has had great influence on furniture design over the past century. This development was based upon what we have termed the artist-craftsman. Something of the variety and nature of these gifted artisans' work appears in the illustrations, whose captions are self-explanatory. The movement arose partly in reaction to the industrialization of the trade during the first half of the 19th century. It also reflected many of the social, and sometimes Socialist, political interests of the time. It sought to promote better design (in its own terms) for the industrial productions. At the same time, it served to foster an exclusive market for specially designed and individually made pieces. In some ways there was nothing new in all this, but the approach was different.

Leading artists, as we have seen, often designed furniture, and since at least the 18th century names of makers had been associated with the finest examples. Yet these were usually that of the owner of the workshop rather than the individual craftsman. Now, ideally at least, the new artist-craftsman was supposed to have created the whole thing from start to finish. Muddled up with all the practical aspects was undoubtedly a reflection of the whole middle-class status clambering of the day. By giving a personal slant to the more expensive pieces, their creators sought not only to give them some parity with the fine arts but also to raise the makers themselves to the more socially acceptable level of painters and sculptors. Other practitioners sought to create and merge themselves into some kind of romantic, idealized, medieval craft guild, in which the romanticism probably played a larger part than history. Little was common to both periods except the fact of handcraftsmanship.

The results were as numerous and as varied as the pastiches had been elsewhere. The few examples by leading makers illustrated here can do little more than draw attention to some general trends of a subject which has only recently received the closer scrutiny of writers and researchers.

The economic explosion in the furniture business at mid-century naturally encouraged the development of mass production to cater to the range of middle classes who now sought self-conscious furnishings to reflect their attitudes as well as to serve practical purposes. Standard designs and standard pieces for the fabrication of which machinery could be devised became a regular feature of the expanding craft. Such manifestations as bentwood furniture evolved. Machines were created to cut and carve, turn legs and arms, plane and dovetail sides and drawers, and all the rest. Though possibly assembled and finished off by hand, such machine-made items poured out all over the world by the thousands. Sometimes manufacturers commissioned artists to design or to adapt for their particular needs, and sometimes the results were not so bad; but for the most part, it was a fairly fortuitous jumble, as if the machines themselves had done whatever their limitations allowed with any of the hordes of historical examples which the current passion for pastiches set before them. This produced a fairly logical reaction among artists and intellectuals, who consciously sought to get away from all this and to promote a return to authentic "craftsmanship" and "handwork." And the tendency is still with us a century later. Whether true or merely at times a romantic notion, something "hand done" is still likely to be regarded as superior to anything that is machine-produced.

For the 19th century, the whole idea was readily

acceptable in line with the current of romantic medievalism so manifest in Scott or Wagner. Thus, a muddled historical imagination could conjure up an idyllic craft-guild happiness to vie with Rousseau's noble savages. The attitude in which England still collected Morland prints and London cries and read cooked-up Arthurian tales evolved a powerful philosophy about such things as the "dignity of labour" in settings where everyone was supposed to have worked in harmony and brotherly amity, and so forth. Such ideas were naturally full meat for a host of nonconformist sympathizers everywhere. So "old-time" guild workshops were established, usually by well-heeled enthusiasts, and all the romanticism of these people was released as they wove and spun, sang madrigals, and joined astonished farm folk in remoter rural areas where junketings such as May Day games and morris dancing still persisted, and their earlier lusty realities may well have been inhibited by the sudden appearance of swooning beauties in long Gothic gowns and beneath parasols. But whatever the reality of factory life and whatever the peasantry might truly have thought of the movement, for a time it swept throughout the Western world.

For many, the plain clean lines of rugged simple wood ousted all the Louis and Renaissance fluff. Gothic—which now meant plain peasant and basic provincial stuff, not the Gothic of pinnacles and crockets, nor certainly the later 16th-century stylistic holdovers or those of about 1750—became the watchword. With an almost cinematic disregard for fact, art school teachers and leading artist-craftsmen created furnishings out of their romanticized ideas of chivalry and Christian rectitude with which, regardless of historical truth, they felt characters like Tristan and King Arthur might have been surrounded in their distant legendary Britain.

In this way, a whole intellectual middle-class revolution started up against the very sources of its prosperity. If the new rich of the first half of the 19th century had set about asserting their own validity against a tradition of feudal privilege, their heirs and successors of the second and third generations, under the leadership of people like William Morris and John Ruskin, sought to make for themselves a new idealized world. In its creation they not only played at a little gentle socialism but, secretly perhaps, felt that their now-established wealth could take the place of noble quarterings. This aim, however, was not achieved in Europe until many decades later.

If Morris has had so much publicity that his name

stands out above others of his era, there were numerous people throughout Europe and in America as well who, if they did not enter so actively into the homespun life, at least encouraged individual designers of the new taste and new trends. Some gave support for the civic art schools that, along with craft centers, were then springing up everywhere. Others aided by giving out direct commissions and awarding scholarships from their factories and offices. Persons, such as Burgess and Mackintosh at Glasgow or Kaare Klint in Denmark, who occupied the new chairs at universities for "arts and crafts" were well prepared to be advocates of fine furnishings as well as of sculpture or painting. The title "Professor" before the author's name became almost a necessity if any book of furniture design was to succeed. These people were immensely influential. For instance, much of the whole Scandinavian movement that has so profoundly affected world styles over the last half century or more depended upon the work of people like Klint. And he himself was not without debt to Sheraton and Hepplewhite, rather more perhaps than to Rossetti or the Nazarenes. Such an attitude obviously influenced the whole approach and status of furniture-makers. The leading academic designers (and in some cases they even made the works themselves or participated directly in some respect, as in the painted pieces by Burne-Jones) became socially acceptable at least within a middle-class intellectual world, and occasionally also by extension to the more emancipated among the upper classes. On the other hand, the status of the ordinary cabinetmaker tended to revert to a lower kind of guild-artisan position. While Chippendale could be accepted, if not as an equal, at least as a significant curiosity by the gentry, few if any of the more ordinary makers of the 19th century would have received this accolade. The design professors might, and even some of the larger-scale manufacturers and purveyors might also—in so far as trade was acceptable at all outside its own circles—but no longer the artisan-craftsman. The "artist-designer" was socially accepted also and, if well-established enough, perhaps the artist-craftsman; but the rest of those involved in the business of furnishings, no. This did not, however, stop the rank and file of better makers from assuming their own opinion of superiority among themselves, judged on the basis of quality of craftsmanship.

What all this combination achieved under the various art movements of the later 19th and early decades of the 20th century we have merely touched upon here in illustration. This is a field of vast potential and excitement for researchers, an area which has as yet been only lightly examined. Until more exhaustive research has been done, a more detailed analysis is difficult and out of place, but even so the illustrations here indicate the general lines of this development. Not least of these—though scarcely as easily applicable as in former centuries—is our opening generalization, which would still seem to hold to some extent: that Northern and more puritan environments instinctively foster reticence, as in Glasgow or in Scandinavia, while ebullience and more florid display are certainly reflected by more Southerly creative spirits such as Antonio Gaudí or Émile Gallé.

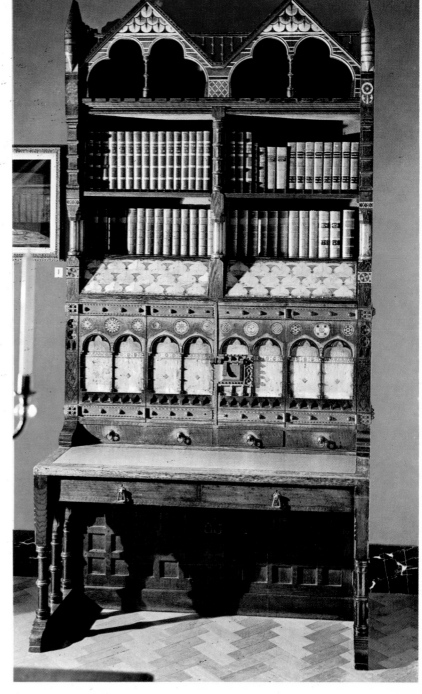

510 *(left)* Cradle of carved oak, painted and gilded. English, c. 1861; designed by Norman Shaw. Victoria and Albert Museum, London.

511 *(above)* Neogothic bureau-bookcase of painted wood. English, exhibited in 1862; designed by Norman Shaw. Victoria and Albert Museum, London.

512 *(below)* Stool of mahogany (copied from an ancient Egyptian model). English, executed in 1884 by Liberty & Company. Victoria and Albert Museum, London.

513 *(right)* Armchair of stained wood with rush seat. English, c. 1865; designed by Dante Gabriel Rossetti and made by Morris & Company. Victoria and Albert Museum, London.

514 *(left)* Leather-covered sofa of mahogany, w ivory inlay. English, c. 1880; designed by Christopher Dresser for Bushloe House, Leicestershire. Victoria and Albert Museum, London.

515 (above) Sideboard of dark-stained wood, with handles of silvered metal and door panels of Japanese paper. English, c. 1867; designed by E. W. Goodwin and made by William Watt. Victoria and Albert Museum, London.

516 (right) Oak armchair, with original upholstery fabric also designed by Morris. English, c. 1883; designed by William Morris. For its era, this chair—with its adjustable backrest—is an example of maximum comfort. Victoria and Albert Museum, London.

517 (above) Mahogany sofa, with original velvet covering. English, probably made c. 1897 by the firm of Liberty & Company. Victoria and Albert Museum, London.

518 (above right) Oak chair. English, c. 1897; by Charles Rennie Mackintosh. Victoria and Albert Museum, London.

519 (right) Rosewood cabinet, inlaid with palisander, tulipwood, and ebony; mounts are of oxidized silver. English, c. 1899; designed by W. A. S. Benson and made by Morris & Company. Victoria and Albert Museum, London.

520 Piano, decorated with painted and gilded gesso.
English, 1883; designed by E. B. Ynes and
made by John Broadwood. The gesso
decoration is by Kate Faulkner.
Victoria and Albert Museum, London.

521 *(right)* Small oak table, stained in ebony
finish. English, c. 1897; made from designs by
Charles Rennie Mackintosh. Glasgow
School of Art.

522 *(below)* Chair of dark-stained wood. English,
1885; designed by E. W. Goodwin and made by
William Watt. Victoria and Albert Museum,
London.

523 *(right)* Occasional table of painted wood.
English, c. 1900; designed by Charles Rennie
Mackintosh. University of Glasgow
(Mackintosh Collection), Glasgow.

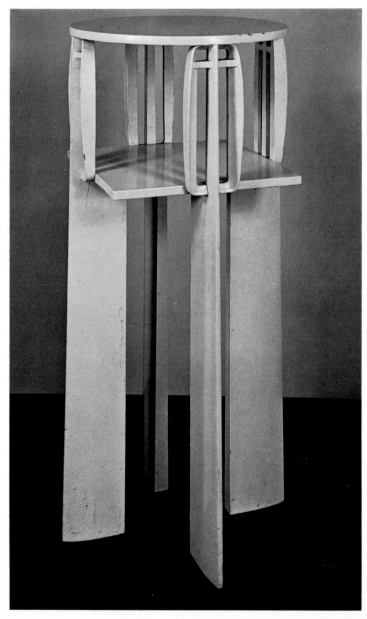

524   Oak cabinet, with copper hinges and silhouette
panel. English, 1896; designed by
C. F. A. Voysey. Victoria and Albert Museum,
London.

525 *(below)* Walnut long-case clock. French, c. 1900; designed by the architect Hector Guimard (who designed the Paris Métro entrances). Musée des Arts Décoratifs, Paris.

526 *(right)* Mahogany display cabinet. German, shown at the Turin World Exhibition in 1902; by Bernhard Pankok. The curious winglike supports are a typical feature of various Pankok designs. Staatliche Museen Preussischer Kulturbesitz, Kunstgewerbemuseum, Berlin.

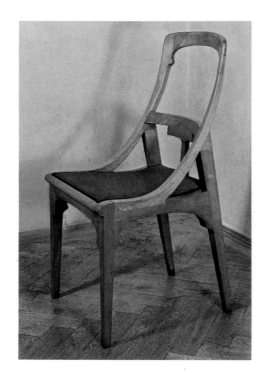

527 *(left)* Chair of light-colored wood, in "Greek" style. German, c. 1900; by Richard Riemerschmid. Stadtmuseum, Munich.

528 *(above)* Writing table of walnut. Italian, c. 1900. Private collection, Milan.

529 *(left)* Walnut secrétaire. Italian, c. 1900. The simple neoclassic lines of this piece are filled in with characteristic serpentine decoration of Art Nouveau—the Italian "stile Liberty" or "gusto floreale." Private collection, Rome.

530 (above) Art Nouveau salon of Maison Gillion-Crowet, Brussels. Belgian, late 19th century. In the background the tracery woodwork by Paul Hankar creates a display cabinet holding vases by Émile Gallé; the furniture in the foreground is by Louis Majorelle. (Photo: P. Hinous, *Connaissance des Arts*)

531 (left) Mahogany armchair, with original embroidered velvet upholstery. French, c. 1900, part of an interior by Louis Majorelle. Galerie Jeanne Fillon, Paris.

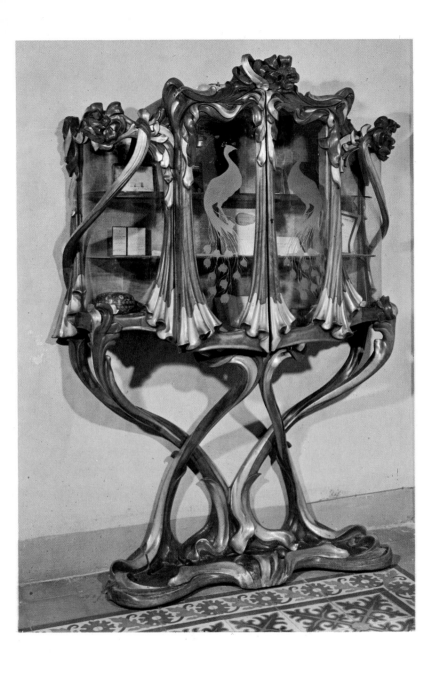

532 *(left)* Walnut display cabinet, partially gilt. Spanish, c. 1900; perhaps designed by the architect Antonio Gaudì. In Spain such Art Nouveau design went under the name "Arte joven." Private collection, Barcelona.

533 *(below)* Small table, inlaid with varied woods on a mahogany base. French, end of 19th century; made by Émile Gallé for the Paris Universal Exposition of 1900. Galerie Alain Lesieutre, Paris.

534 *(above)* Walnut sideboard. French, end of
19th century; made by Eugène Gaillard as part
of furnishings for the Bing pavilion at Paris
Universal Exposition of 1900. Museum für
Kunst under Gewerbe, Hamburg.
(Photo: Kleinhempel)

535 *(below)* Sofa with frame of palisander and
original upholstery. French, 1911; by Eugène
Gaillard (pendant to another divan in the
Musée des Arts Décoratifs, Paris). Galerie
Alain Lesieutre, Paris.

316

536 *(left)* Carved wooden chair, with leather seat. French, end of 19th century; similar to an example designed by Eugène Gaillard for the Bing pavilion at the Paris Universal Exposition of 1900. Musée des Arts Décoratifs, Paris.

537 *(above)* Leather-upholstered bench. French, c. 1900; by Eugène Gaillard. Musée des Arts Décoratifs, Paris.

538 *(below)* Small mahogany table, with detail of inlaid top. French, end of 19th century; signed by Émile Gallé. A similar example by the same designer in the Kunstgewerbemuseum of Berlin is dated 1898. The delicate inlay has a pattern of swallows and stylized foliage. Collection of Doctor Virgilio Gaddi, Florence.

539 *(above)* Oak furniture suite. English, c. 1901;
by Charles Rennie Mackintosh. An interesting
feature here is the backrests which extend
uninterrupted to the floor. Victoria and Albert
Museum, London.

540 *(right)* Writing desk of stained oak. Austrian,
c. 1905; by Josef Hoffmann. This small desk
exhibits the severe geometric forms typical of
the Vienna Sezession designers.
Österreichisches Museum für Angewandte
Kunst, Vienna.

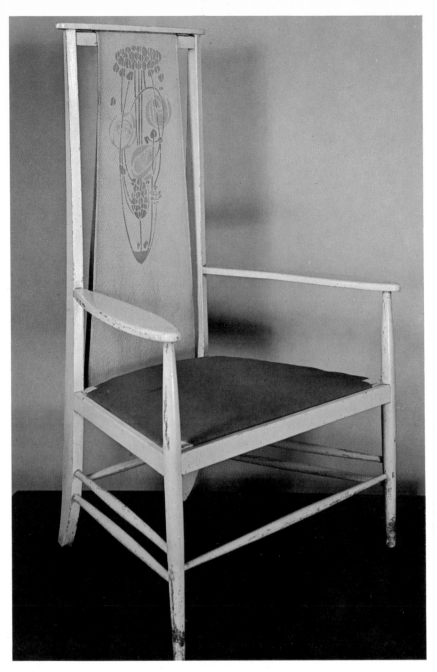

541 *(above)* Armchair of lacquered wood.
English, early 20th century; by or in the style
of Charles Rennie Mackintosh. University of
Glasgow (Mackintosh Collection), Glasgow.

542 *(right)* Oak armchair. English, c. 1909;
attributed to C. F. A. Voysey. Victoria and
Albert Museum, London.

543 *(above)* Coffer, with Swedish birch veneer and ebony and mahogany inlay. Austrian, c. 1906; designed by Josef Hoffmann. The stylized geometric decoration here typifies the style of this leader in the Vienna Sezession. Österreichisches Museum für Angewandte Kunst, Vienna.

544 *(right)* Reading stand of elm (one of a pair). French, 1901; by the sculptor-decorator Alexandre Charpentier. The Art Nouveau love of vegetal forms is expressed with exquisite rhythm and skill here. Musée des Arts Décoratifs, Paris.

Bibliography

Aslin, Elizabeth, *19th Century English Furniture*, London, 1962.

Baillie, G. H., *Watchmakers and Clockmakers of the World*, 2nd ed., London, 1947.

Bajot, Edouard, *Encyclopédie du meuble, du XV siècle jusqu'à nos jours*, 7 vols., Paris, 1901–09.

Bell, J. Munroe, *The Furniture Designs of Chippendale, Hepplewhite and Sheraton, arranged by J. Munroe Bell*, New York, 1938.

Benn, R. Davis, *Style in Furniture*, London, 1904.

Berendsen, Anne, *Het nederlandse interieur*, Utrecht, 1950.

Bjerkoe, Ethel Hall, *Cabinetmakers of America*, New York, 1957.

Boger, Louise Ade, *The Complete Guide to Furniture Styles*, New York, 1959.

Bolton, Arthur T., *The Architecture of Robert Adam and James Adam (1758–1794)*, 2 vols., London, 1922.

Brackett, Oliver, *English Furniture Illustrated, A Pictorial Review of English Furniture from Chaucer to Queen Victoria*, London, 1950 (rev. and ed., H. Clifford Smith).

Brackett, Oliver, *Thomas Chippendale*, London, 1924.

Brentano's, New York, *The Interior Decorative Art of France in the 17th and 18th Centuries*, 2 vols., New York, 1917.

Bridenbaugh, Carl, *The Colonial Craftsman*, New York, 1950.

Brosio, Valentino, *Ambienti italiani dell'Ottocento*, Milan, 1963.

Brosio, Valentino, *Mobili italiani dell'Ottocento*, Milan, 1962.

Brunhammer, Yvonne, and de Fayet, Monique, *Meubles et ensembles époques Régence et Louis XV; Meubles et ensembles époque Louis XVI; Meubles et ensembles époques Directoire et Empire*, 4 vols., Paris, 1965.

Bueno, Luis Perez, *El meuble*, new ed., Barcelona, 1950.

Burgess, Fred W., *Antique Furniture*, London, 1915.

Burr, Grace Hardendorff, *Hispanic Furniture, with Examples in the Collection of the Hispanic Society of America*, New York, 1941 (enlarged ed., 1964).

Byne, Arthur, and Byne, Mildred Stapley, *Spanish Interiors and Furniture*, 3 vols., New York, 1921.

Cescinsky, Herbert, *English Furniture of the Eighteenth Century*, 3 vols., London, 1909–1911.

Champeaux, Alfred de, *Le meuble*, 2 vols., Paris, 1885.

Cherikover, L. Z., *Bykovaka mebel' russkogo klassitsizma kontsa XVIII nachala XIX v.v.*, Moscow, 1954.

Chippendale, Thomas, *The Gentleman and Cabinet-Maker's Director, being a Collection of the Most Elegant and Useful Designs of Household Furniture in the Most Fashionable Taste*, 1st ed., 1754; 2nd ed., 1755; 3rd ed., 1762, London.

Clouston, R. S., *English Furniture and Furniture Makers of the Eighteenth Century*, London, 1906.

Cole, Herbert, *An Introduction to the Period Styles of England and France, with a Chapter on the Dutch Renaissance*, Manchester, 1927.

Coleridge, Anthony, *The Chippendale Period in English Furniture*, London, 1966.

Collection Connaissance des Arts, *Grands artisans d'autrefois: Les ébénistes du XVIII° siècle français*, Paris, 1963.

Collection Connaissance des Arts, *Le XVII° siècle français*, Paris, 1958.

Comstock, Helen, *American Furniture: Seventeenth, Eighteenth, and Nineteenth Century Styles*, New York, 1962.

Cornelius, Charles O., *Early American Furniture*, New York, 1926.

Cornelius, Charles O., *Furniture Masterpieces of Duncan Phyfe*, New York, 1922.

Dacier, Emile, *Le style Louis XVI*, Paris, 1939.

Del Puglia, Raffaella, *Mobili e ambienti italiani dal gotico al floreale*, 2 vols., Milan, 1963.

Destailleur, Hippolyte Alexandre Gabriel Walter, *Recueil d'estampes relatives à l'ornamentation des apartments aux XVI, XVII, et XVIII siècles*, 2 vols., Paris, 1863–1871.

Dilke, Lady, *French Decoration and Furniture in the 18th Century*, London, 1901.

Downs, Joseph, *American Furniture, Queen Anne and Chippendale Periods*, New York, 1952.

Drepperd, Carl, *American Clocks and Clockmakers*, New York, 1955.

Drepperd, Carl, *Handbook of Antique Chairs*, New York, 1948.

Dreyfus, Carle, *French Furniture in the Louvre Museum* (Louis XIV and Louis XV pieces), Paris, 1921.

Dumonthier, Ernest, *Les siéges de Georges Jacob, époques Louis XV, Louis XVI et Révolutionnaire*, Paris, 1922.

Dutton, Ralph, *The English Interior, 1500–1900*, London, 1948.

Dyer, Walter Alden, *Early American Craftsmen*, New York, 1915.

Edwards, Ralph, *English Chairs*, London, 1965.

Edwards, Ralph, *The Shorter Dictionary of English Furniture from the Middle Ages to the Late Georgian Period*, London, 1964.

Edwards, Ralph, and Jourdain, Margaret, *Georgian Cabinet-makers c. 1700–1800*, rev. ed., London, 1955.

Ellwood, George Montague, *English Furniture and Decoration, 1660–1800*, London, 1909.

Enriques, Maria Dolores, *El mueble español en los siglos XV, XVI y XVII*, Madrid, 1951.

Fastnedge, Ralph, *English Furniture Styles from 1500 to 1830*, London, 1954.

Fayet, Monique de, *Meubles et ensembles, renaissance espagnole*, Paris, 1961.

Feduchi, Luis M., *El mueble en España*, Madrid, 1949–1950.

Floud, Peter, *The Connoisseur Period Guides, The Early Victorian Period 1830–1860*, London, 1958.

Floud, Peter, *The Concise Encyclopaedia of Antiques*, vol. III, London, 1957.

Foley, Edwin, *The Book of Decorative Furniture, its Form, Colours and History*, 2 vols., London, 1911.

Gloag, John, *English Furniture*, 5th ed., London, 1965.

Gloag, John, *The Englishman's Chair*, London, 1964.

Gloag, John, *A Short Dictionary of Furniture*, London, 1954.

Guilmard, Désiré, *Les maîtres ornementistes*, 2 vols., Paris, 1880–1881.

Guimaraes, Alfredo, and Sardoeira, Albano, *Mobiliário artistico português*, vol. I; *Lamego*, Opôrto, 1924.

Halsey, R. T. H.; Cornelius, C. O.; and Downs, J., *Handbook of the American Wing, Metropolitan Museum*, 7th ed., 1942.

Harris, Eileen, *The Furniture of Robert Adam*, London, 1963.

Harris, John, *Regency Furniture Designs from Contemporary Source Books, 1803–1826*, London, 1961.

Havard, Henry, *Dictionnaire de l'ameublement et de la décoration depuis le XIII* siècle jusqu'à nos jours*, 4 vols., Paris, 1887–1890.

Hayward, J. F., *English Cabinets*, London, 1964.

Hayward, J. F., *Tables*, London, 1961.

Heal, Sir Ambrose, *London Furniture Makers, From the Restoration to the Victorian Era, 1660–1840*, London, 1953.

Hepplewhite, A. and Co., *The Cabinet Maker and Upholsterer's Guide*, 1st ed., 1788; 2nd ed., 1789; 3rd ed., 1794, London.

Honour, Hugh, *Chinoiserie, The Vision of Cathay*, London, 1961.

Hornor, William MacPherson, *Blue Book of Philadelphia Furniture, William Penn to George Washington*, Philadelphia, 1935.

Hunter, George Leland, *Italian Furniture and Interiors*, 2 vols., New York, 1918.

Iverson, Marion Day, *The American Chair 1630–1890*, New York, 1957.

Jacquemart, Albert, *A History of Furniture*, London, 1878.

Janneau, Guillaume, *Les meubles*, 3 vols., Paris, 1929.

Jessen, Peter, *Meister des Ornamentichs*, Berlin, 1923.

Jessen, Peter, *Der Ornamentatich*, Berlin, 1920.

Jonge, C. H. de, and Vogelsang, W., *Holländische Möbel und Raumkunst von 1650–1780*, The Hague, 1922.

Jourdain, Margaret, *English Interior Decoration 1500–1830*, London, 1950.

Jourdain, Margaret, *Regency Furniture, 1795–1820*, London, 1948.

Jourdain, Margaret, *The Work of William Kent*, London, 1948.

Jourdain, Margaret, and Rose, T., *English Furniture, The Georgian Period, 1750–1830*, London, 1953.

Joy, E. T., *The Country Life Book of English Furniture*, London, 1964.

Joy, E. T., *English Furniture A. D. 43–1950*, London, 1962.

Kimball, Fiske, *The Creation of the Rococo*, Philadelphia, 1943.

Kreisel, Heinrich, *Fränkische Rokokomöbel*, Darmstadt, 1956.

Layton, Edwin J., *Thomas Chippendale*, London, 1928.

Ledoux-Lebard, Denise, *Les ébénistes parisiens, 1795–1830*, Paris, 1951.

Lenygon, Francis, *The Decoration and Furniture of English Mansions during the 17th and 18th Centuries*, London, 1909.

Levy, Saul, *Il mobile veneziano del Settecento*, Milan, 1964.

Litchfield, Frederick, *History of Furniture, From the Earliest to the Present Time*, 7th ed., London, 1922.

Lockwood, L. V., *Colonial Furniture in America*, 2 vols., New York.

McClelland, Nancy Vincent, *Duncan Phyfe and the English Regency, 1795–1830*, New York, 1939.

Macquoid, Percy, *A History of English Furniture*, 4 vols., London, 1904–1908.

Macquoid, Percy, and Edwards, Ralph, *The Dictionary of English Furniture, from the Middle Ages to the Late Georgian Period*, 3 vols., London, 1954.

Madsen, Tschudi, *Sources of Art Nouveau*, Oslo, 1956.

Maillard, Elisa *Old French Furniture and Its Surroundings, 1610–1815*, London, 1925.

Martin, Henry, *Le style Louis XIV*, Paris, 1947.

Metropolitan Museum of Art, *American Chippendale Furniture, A Picture Book*, New York, 1950.

Miller, Edgar George, Jr., *American Antique Furniture*, 2 vols., Baltimore, 1937.

Milne, James Lees, *The Age of Adam*, London, 1947.

Molinier, Emile, *Royal Interiors and Decorations of the 17th and 18th Centuries*, 5 vols., Paris, 1902.

Morazzoni, Giuseppe, *Ambienti italiani del Seicento*, Milan, 1964.

Morazzoni, Giuseppe, *Il mobile veneziano*, Milan, 1958.

Morazzoni, Giuseppe, *Il mobile neoclassico italiano*, Milan, 1955.

Morazzoni, Giuseppe, *Il mobile genovese*, Milan, 1949.

Morazzoni, Giuseppe, *Il mobilio italiano*, Florence, 1940.

Morris & Co., *Catalogues of Tapestries, Wall-papers, Fabrics, Furniture, Upholstery, and Decoration, before and after 1900*.

Mostra del barocco piemontese, mobili e intagli (catalogue), ed. by Vittorio Viale, Turin, 1964.

Musgrave, Clifford, *Regency Furniture*, London, 1961.

Nagel, Charles, *American Furniture 1650–1850*, 1949.

Nutting, Wallace, *Furniture Treasury*, 3 vols., New York, 1948–1949.

Nutting, Wallace, *The Clock Book*, New York, 1935.

Odom, William M., *A History of Italian Furniture from the 14th to the Early 19th Centuries*, 2 vols., New York, 1918.

Ormsbee, Thomas H., *Field Guide to American Victorian Furniture*, Boston, 1951.

Ormsbee, Thomas H., *Early American Furniture Makers*, New York, 1930.

Palmer, Brooks, *The Book of American Clocks*, New York, 1950.

Pedrini, Augusto, *Italian Furniture; Interiors and Decoration of the 15th and 16th Centuries*, London, 1949.

Pevsner, Nikolaus, *High Victorian Design, A Study of the Exhibits of 1851*, London, 1951.

Pignatti, Terisio, *Mobili italiani del Rinascimento*, Milan, 1961.

Pignatti, Terisio, *Lo stile dei mobili*, Milan, 1951.

Piranesi, Giovanni, *Diverse maniere d'adornare i camini*, Rome, 1767.

Pluym, William van der, *Vijf eeuwen binnenhuis en meubels in Nederland, 1450–1950*, Amsterdam, 1954.

Pratt, Richard, *Second Treasury of Early American Homes*, New York, 1954.

Pugin, Augustus W. N., *Gothic Furniture in the Style of the 15th Century, Designed and Etched by A. W. N. Pugin*, London, 1835.

Ricci, Seymour de, *Louis XIV and Regency Furniture and Decoration*, London, 1929.

Ricci, Seymour de, *Louis XVI Furniture*, London, 1913.

Ries, Estelle H., *American Rugs*, Cleveland, 1950.

Roe, F. Gordon, *Victorian Furniture*, New York, 1952.

Rogers, John C., *English Furniture*, rev. ed., London, 1950.

Saglio, André, *French Furniture*, London, 1907.

Salverte, François, Comte de, *Les ébénistes du XVIIIᵉ siècle, leurs oeuvres et leurs marques*, Paris, 1937.

Schmitz, Hermann, *Deutsche Möbel des Barock und Rokoko*, Stuttgart, 1923.

Schmutzler, Robert, *Art Nouveau*, London, 1964.

Sheraton, Thomas, *The Cabinet-Maker, Upholsterer and General Artist's Encyclopaedia* (Unfinished), London, 1805.

Sheraton, Thomas, *The Cabinet Dictionary, Containing an Explanation of All the Terms Used in the Cabinet, Chair and Upholstery Branches, with Directions for Varnishing, Polishing and Gilding*, London, 1803.

BIBLIOGRAPHY

Sheraton, Thomas, *The Cabinet-Maker and Upholsterer's Drawing Book*, published in four parts from 1791–1794; 3rd ed., London, 1802.

Singleton, Esther, *Dutch and Flemish Furniture*, London, 1907.

Souchal G., *Le mobilier français au XVIIIᵉ siècle*, Paris, 1934.

Speltz, Alexander, *Styles of Ornament, from Prehistoric Times to the Middle of the XIXth Century*, rev. transl., London, 1910.

Strange, Thomas Arthur, *French Interiors, Furniture, Decoration, Woodwork and Allied Arts, 17th, 18th, 19th Centuries*, London, 1907.

Symonds, R. W., *Furniture Making in the Seventeenth and Eighteenth Century in England*, London, 1955.

Symonds, R. W., *A Book of English Clocks*, London, 1947.

Symonds, R. W., *Masterpieces of English Furniture and Clocks; A Study of Mahogany and Walnut Furniture*, London, 1940.

Tattersall, C. E. C., and Lewis, F., *A History of British Carpets*, Leigh-on-Sea, 1934.

Terni de Gregory, Winifred, *Vecchi mobili italiani; Tipo in uso dal secolo XV al secolo XX*, Milan, 1953.

Tinti, Mario, *Il mobilio fiorentino*, Milan, 1929.

Vallance, Aymer, *The Art of William Morris*, London, 1897.

Vardy, John, *Selection from the Works of Inigo Jones and William Kent*, London, 1744.

Verlet, Pierre, *Le style Louis XV*, Paris, 1942.

Viaux, Jacqueline, *Le meuble en France*, Paris, 1962.

Victoria and Albert Museum, *A History of English Furniture*, London, 1955.

Vogelsang, Willem, *Le meuble hollandais au Musée Nationale d'Amsterdam*, The Hague, 1910.

Wallace Collection Catalogue on Furniture, London, 1956.

Ward-Jackson, Peter, *English Furniture Designs of the Eighteenth Century*, London, 1959.

Watson, F. J. B., *Louis XVI Furniture*, London, 1960.

Weigert, R. A., *Le style Louis XIV*, Paris, 1941.

Wernitz, G. (ed.), *Historische Möbel und Inneräume*, Berlin, 1956.

Index of Names

in picture captions